Feng Shui Chic

Stylish Designs for Harmonious Living

Feng Shui Chic

Stylish Designs for Harmonious Living

Sharon Stasney

Sterling Publishing Co., Inc. New York

A Sterling/Chapelle Book

Chapelle, Ltd.:

- Owner: Jo Packham
- Editor: Laura Best
- Photography: Scott Zimmerman, Scott Zimmerman Photography
   Kevin Dilley, Hazen Photography
- Illustrations: Areta Bingham, Amber Fuller
- Staff: Ann Bear, Kass Burchett, Marilyn Goff,
   Holly Hollingsworth, Susan Jorgensen,
   Barbara Milburn, Linda Orton, Karmen Quinney,
   Leslie Ridenour, Cindy Stoeckl, Gina Swapp, Sara Toliver

If you have any questions or comments, please contact:
   Chapelle, Ltd., Inc., P.O. Box 9252, Ogden, UT 84409
   (801) 621-2777 • (801) 621-2788 Fax
   e-mail: chapelle@chapelleltd.com
   website: chapelleltd.com

Library of Congress Cataloging-in-Publication Data

Stasney, Sharon.
   Feng Shui Chic : stylish designs for harmonious living / Sharon Stasney.
      p. cm.
   Includes index.
   ISBN 0-8069-6081-7
   1. Feng-shui. I. Title.

   BF1779.F4 S79 2000
   133.3'337--dc21   00-037285

10 9 8 7 6 5 4 3

Published by Sterling Publishing Company, Inc.
387 Park Avenue South, New York, NY 10016
©2000 by Sharon Stasney
Distributed in Canada by Sterling Publishing
c/o Canadian Manda Group, One Atlantic Avenue, Suite 105
Toronto, Ontario, Canada M6K 3E7
Distributed in Great Britain and Europe by Cassell PLC
Wellington House, 125 Strand, London WCR2 0BB, England
Distributed in Australia by Capricorn Link (Australia) Pty Ltd.
P.O. Box 6651, Baulkham Hills, Business Centre, NSW 2153, Australia
Printed in China
All Rights Reserved

Sterling ISBN 0-8069-6081-7

Introduction

Feng shui (pronounced fung schway) is thousands of years old, yet it is also today's latest design trend. Feng shui design is just as effective today as it was in Royal China because it is based on fundamental principles of how to create different energy states in the human body.

Every design choice generates a physical and emotional response in your body. Your choices can encourage you to slow down, relax, get creative, express enthusiasm, feel grounded and secure—whatever you need from your space. You do not need to incorporate Asian decor items to benefit from feng shui. Whatever your decorating style, feng shui principles will help you design a home you want to live in.

Table of Contents

Applying feng shui principles to your home can:
▲ Open you to new experiences.
▲ Enhance relaxation/ rejuvenation.
▲ Stabilize your moods.
▲ Encourage creativity/ confidence in family.
▲ Encourage focus on detailed tasks.
▲ Increase intimacy in your relationships.
▲ Strengthen immune system/energy levels.
▲ Help you let go of unwanted clutter.
▲ Bring balance/harmony into your home/life.

How it all works

Your relationship to home

Your home is a powerful force in your life. Every day it offers a greater understanding of who you are and what your life is currently focused on. Your relationships with abundance, health, intimacy, creativity, and family are mirrored on your walls, ingrained in your tables, and reflected in your pictures. Home is where you physically manifest your beliefs about the world.

However, your home is more than just a mirror; it is a dynamic force that is constantly responding to the intentions of those who live in it. Your home affects you just as you affect it. The colors, patterns, and structures with which you surround yourself generate energetic vibrations that may or may not serve you. A depressed person, for example, might create a home in which everything is low to the ground, dark, and slow-moving. Such an environment, besides being a reflection of the person's mental and emotional state, will physically re-create depressed states in a person's body every day. The good news is that changing the decor of the home could change a person's energy in a healing way. Physically shifting elements in your space shifts the way energy flows through your body.

Your home is an active force in your life, regardless of whether or not you attend to it. By becoming aware of how your home mirrors you, and how to shift its energy, you can turn your home into a force that heals, restores balance, and encourages growth. Feng shui is the art of consciously making design choices that support your life's path.

Integrating feng shui in your own way

You can integrate feng shui into your design choices on many different levels, depending on what resonates with you. Each design choice has a physical aspect (the color blue relaxes the muscles and can lower your heart rate and blood pressure), a psychological/emotional aspect (the color blue might depress you), a cultural aspect (bright blue doors are considered cheerful in Sante Fe but obnoxious in Boston).

Many traditional feng shui adjustments originate in a cultural and symbolic system (Royal China) that may not work for you. Once you understand the intent of each adjustment, you can modify the traditional adjustments to match your own cultural and personal symbolic system.

This book will explain the energetic intent of feng shui adjustments and provide guidance on implementing adjustments that work on multiple levels simultaneously. It is important to use only those adjustments that make sense to you and resonate with your intention for your home. Placing something in your home that you don't like just because it is "good feng shui" will not enhance your home or support your personal growth.

Chi

Feng shui design is based on the awareness that an electromagnetic energy flows around and through your body, linking you to every other person, object, and force in the universe.

Chi is the Chinese term for this universal life force that reminds us of the underlying connected nature of all things. You feel this energetic connection to others when someone walks into the room behind you and you feel the presence without turning around. Or perhaps you have walked into a room where two people are arguing. Even if they fall silent, the energy of their angry words hangs in the air. Sometimes this heavy chi can remain for days if it is not cleared.

Chi moves and changes form constantly. The chi in a human body transfers to the external environment and vice versa. Imagine sitting in a leather chair on a cold winter day. The chair is cold and does not radiate energy. After you sit in the chair for a while though, the heat energy from your body is transferred to the chair and the chair begins to give it back to you.

Feng Shui Chic will provide exercises and opportunities for exploring how chi feels in your body (personal chi) and how radically your personal chi changes based on environment. After you make feng shui adjustments, you can measure the effectiveness in a meaningful way.

The energy field surrounding the body is called the aura.

Your aura

Personal chi is the interface between your body's energy and the environment's energy. Personal chi is often referred to as the "aura." The size and shape of your aura change constantly. Generally, you extend your aura when you feel comfortable, safe, or happy. This makes you seem more approachable to others.

Fearful, unhappy, or discomforting states typically cause you to retract your auric field, pull it in closer around you. The sensation known as "withdrawal" happens when you retract your energy so that your auric field no longer overlaps the other person's field. They feel the withdrawal of your personal chi.

You are constantly expanding and contracting your aura due to interpersonal and environmental triggers. Feng shui will help you be more aware of how your physical environment influences your aura.

As you sit reading *Feng Shui Chic*, extend your awareness to the energy surrounding your body. How comfortable are you sitting in your chair? Do you feel supported? Protected? Comfortable? Get a sense of how far around you your energy extends. Now, pick up your chair (if it is one you can lift) and set it right in the middle of a doorway. As you now sit in the chair, notice how your aura changes. Did you extend it further, indicating a greater sense of comfort and safety, or did you contract it? Obviously the size and type of chair will also make a difference in how you feel sitting in it. With feng shui, you realize that everything from position to color, to shape, to texture, effects your energy.

Flowers, bricks, wood, rocks every organic force has chi.

Feeling energy move between your hands helps you experience energy, rather than just read about it.

1. Hold the rods loosely around the base, so they swing freely. Keep hands about shoulder-width apart, parallel to the floor. Tell the rods (either mentally or out loud) to go straight ahead. This grounds your own energy field, sending it down into the earth and helps you become more neutral. Instead of picking up shifts in your energy, the rods can now measure the shifts in the environment.

2. Once you find neutral, you can ask yes or no questions. When you think yes, the rods will cross in front, when you think no they will spread out.

Feeling chi between your hands

A starting point in working with energy is to feel the chi between your hands. The palms have chakras (places in the body where chi concentrates), and it is often easier to feel energy there.

Stand with your feet shoulder-width apart, elbows bent, hands parallel with the floor facing each other. Clench your hands into fists a couple of times to get the blood flowing to that part of your body. Then raise your hands to shoulder height, spreading them out further than your shoulders, and slowly start to bring them together. It helps to visualize holding a round ball of energy between your hands. As you bring them closer, you will begin to feel a tingling sensation between your hands, especially at the fingertips.

As you continue to push this energy in and pull it back out again (without letting your hands touch), it starts to feel like strong magnets are pulling your hands together whenever they get close.

Using dowsing rods to measure chi

Another way to measure shifts in chi is to use dowsing rods. Dowsers have used these L-shaped rods for centuries to find water and pockets of geopathic stress. (Geopathic stress pockets occur when intense volatile energies under the earth's crust bubble up to the surface, creating areas where the energy is not healthy for human beings.)

You can use dowsing rods to find the edge of an energy field, see where chi builds up in your space, or understand your own energetic response to different placements. Dowsing rods are helpful because they help you visually perceive shifts in your personal chi. The more senses you activate in understanding chi, the more energy work becomes a part of your reality.

3. To use the rods to locate shifts in energy, walk slowly through your space watching where the rods spread apart.

If you have someone with you, use the rods to measure the size of his aura and see what happens when he stands in different positions. Holding the rods in front of you in the neutral position, walk very slowly toward the person. When the rods hit the edge of the person s auric field, they will spread out.

Now have the person turn around so his back is to you and walk toward him again. Notice how much smaller his aura is when his back is turned to you. This is because he pulls his aura in tighter around his body to protect himself when he s in a vulnerable position.

You can use dowsing rods to gauge the impact of your environment on your chi as well. Stand against a solid wall and have your friend hold the rods to measure the edge of your aura. Now stand in front of a sharp edge, such as the edge of a table, or a sharp corner where two walls come together. Notice what happens to your aura.

When walking into the path of a mirror, dowsing rods typically spread out. This is because a mirror activates the surrounding area. Place seating to the side of a mirror, rather than directly in front to avoid the strong chi flow of the mirror.

Chi & the chakras

The chakra system is the Vedic system of understanding how energy flows in the body. A chakra is a place in the body where energy concentrates. The seven major chakras are located starting at the base of the spine and running up the spine to the crown of the head.

First chakra

The first chakra is referred to as the root chakra and is located at the base of the spine. It governs our fight/flight mechanism and is primarily concerned with safety, tribal support, and our place in the physical world. The color of the root chakra is red, preferably a deep maroon and deep earthy browns. It aligns with the element of earth in feng shui five-element theory.

Second chakra

The second chakra is located in the reproductive organs. It governs sexuality, interactions with another being, our sense of a social self, our attachments to money, and our need to "control" others, ourselves, or situations. Its color is primarily orange, but it is also associated with pink. It aligns with water in five-element theory.

Third chakra

The third chakra is your center of personal power. It is your source of will power and influence. It is located in the solar plexus (the stomach area). When someone takes a jab at you (physically or emotionally) you feel a sharp intake of energy in your stomach. When your third chakra energy is weak, you experience the phenomena of butterflies in your stomach. This airy, spinning sensation makes it difficult to assert yourself or present yourself in a forceful way. It is usually harder to stand up for your rights or feel a strong sense of self-esteem if your third chakra is weak. Its color is yellow. It aligns itself with fire in five-element theory.

Fourth chakra

The fourth chakra is the heart center, the source of unconditional love and compassion for others, and the ability to forgive and let go of grievances. This chakra is the central point that balances the energies of the lower three chakras, which are concerned with the well-being of the individual, and with the higher three chakras, which are more cosmic and universal in nature. It is the center of healing energies, healing both body and spirit. Its color is green and its physical location in the body is the heart space. It aligns itself with earth in five-element theory.

Fifth chakra

The fifth chakra is the voice chakra, located at the throat. It is the center of shifting from a personal power base to a spiritual one. The energy of the fifth chakra opens your connection to a guiding force beyond your personal means. You move from thinking that you have to do it all to aligning yourself with this guiding power, whatever form that power takes for you. The ability to trust a guiding power always comes from feeling the healing love of the universe, therefore, the fifth chakra follows the fourth. Someone with strong fifth chakra energy is able to let go of personal attachments and open up to a more universal sense of self. Its color is blue. It aligns itself with wood in five-element theory.

There are many books explaining how energy moves through the chakras. *Feng Shui Chic* uses this system to explain how different feng shui adjustments affect different parts of the body, which in turn affect different life aspects. The basic associations between the major seven chakras, body locations, and life aspects are included below.

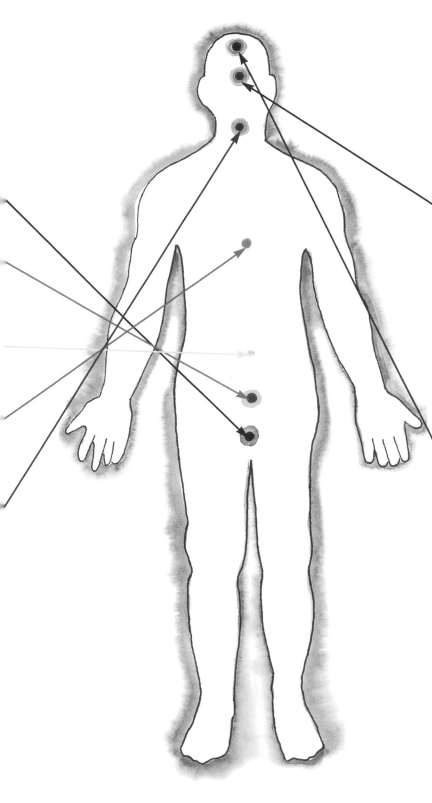

Sixth chakra

The sixth chakra is the third eye or intuitive presence. It is located between the eyebrows. It is an opening to cosmic energies and an acceptance of intuitive messages and guidance. It is the power of the mind and the seat of emotional intelligence. Although the mind is often disdained as a disruptive and disquieting influence, it is a primary way in which we make sense of our world. We think about things. Strong fifth chakra energy means a clear mind, an absence of confusion and scattered jumbled thinking. Its color is indigo. It aligns itself with metal in five-element theory.

Seventh chakra

The seventh chakra is the crown chakra, located at the top of the head and extending up above the body. It is the seat of our spiritual nature as human beings, our connection to divine light and guidance. It governs the interface between this world and other realms of existence. People that communicate with spiritual guides or angels and have a clairvoyance of future or past events, have a strong energy flow in their seventh chakra. Its colors are violet and gold. It aligns with the fire element.

14

The symbols you place in your home shift your energy. The buddha represents peace and compassion.

Yin & yang in balance

The chi that flows through the earth, the heavens, and your body, moves in two general forms. We describe these forms of movement as yin and yang, the receptive and the creative.

The yin/yang dichotomy divides energy into opposites that attract their opposite. This attraction creates movement. We need to balance this interaction between yin and yang to keep energy flowing at the right pace in our lives.

Too much yin energy, and movement slows, chi stagnates, the body shuts down, and ill health results. Too much yang, and chi speeds along too quickly, life changes rapidly, and one's blood pressure and heart rate rise, again resulting in ill health.

When designing your home, balancing these two forces can return you to a state of balance and wholeness. Shifting the yin/yang balance of your home can generate physical, mental, and emotional healing.

Before you start moving furniture around, however, it is important to first ascertain whether the people living in the home have a stronger yin or a stronger yang force in their bodies. Based on this assessment, you can balance the environment and the body.

In this room, the black furniture (yin) balances the yang force of the yellow walls. The upward-reaching plants and corner light bring energy up while the heavy square fireplace adds stability, keeping all in balance.

Personal chi assessment

No one is entirely yin or yang, but at any given point in time you have a predominant energy in your body. You will notice that this energy shifts with the seasons, the time of day, or even food choices. This is important because what you need from your home will change according to seasons, times of day, and moods. As your body shifts, so must your space. Start with how you are feeling today. Check the attributes in each list below that describe you in the present moment and count up the score. Once you tally your yin and yang attributes, you will have a pretty good idea of where you fit in the spectrum.

Yang attributes

Light
Confident
Enthusiastic
Logical
Outgoing
Strong
Direct, focused
Quick movements
Exuberant
Mental, intellectual
Value decisiveness & change

Yin attributes

Heavy
Sensitive
Gentle
Imaginative
Introspective
Soft
Nurturing
Slow movements
Quiet
Physically oriented
Value comfort & safety

Too much Yang

Feel hyperactive
Do not express emotions easily
Energetic & active
Always thinking about the future
Not practical enough
Wander through life
Have a hard time staying home
Throw everything away

Too much Yin

Get depressed often
Cry frequently
Gain weight easily
Dwell on the past
Feelings of hopelessness
Tend to control others
Do not want to leave the house
Hold on to things too long

Yin decor adjustments

Shapes

Include curved or flowing shapes. Exchanging a sturdy wood coffee table for a curvy wicker one will shift the balance from yang to yin. Build in slopes, terraces, or cascading effects with garden beds, curtains, or candles. The circle is an exception; although it is curved, it spins energy outward and is, therefore, yang.

Colors

Tone it down. Deep dark colors, muddy tones (brick red, sage green), soft pastels, and muted hues all increase yin energy in the home. Black is the most yin color of all, pulling energy inward. Stay away from sharp white walls and bouncy yellow if you want to increase yin energy.

Furnishings

Soften & absorb. Although mirrors make great feng shui cures, too many mirrors create an intensely yang space. Swap wood furniture for upholstered versions, get rid of the metal table base with the round glass top, add paper screens and large cushions, cover the table with a cloth. Another way to create a yin vibration is to choose furniture and decor items that are low to the ground. Hanging pictures lower than eye level will also move energy down.

Lighting

Think soft. Soften overhead lights by installing dimmer switches. Get full window coverings. Increase yin by adding hanging lamps and downward lamp lighting.

Windows & floor treatments

Rich & full. Rich textures slow down the chi flow. For windows, move from wood shutters to drapes, or from metal mini blinds to folded roman shades. For flooring, cover that tile floor or marble entryway with thick rugs or rush matting. And remember, wood floors are nice, but a plush carpet softens an agitated mind and absorbs excess stress.

Density & size

Fill it up. The more furniture you fit into a space, the denser and more yin the space becomes. If you need more stability, you can anchor a room with large, heavy items such as an armoire, a chest, or a buffet. In the kitchen, anchor light-colored countertops by placing something heavy such as pottery or a potted plant in the corners.

16

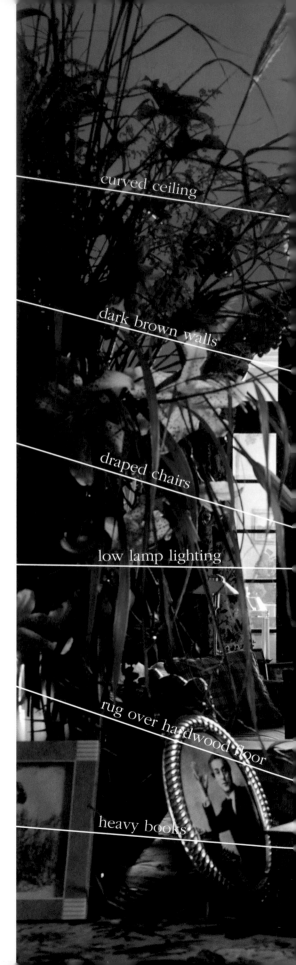

curved ceiling

dark brown walls

draped chairs

low lamp lighting

rug over hardwood floor

heavy books

Yang decor adjustments

Shapes

Straighten up. A straight vertical line will remind you to stand up for yourself and ask for what you want. Triangles and pyramids are dynamic and motivating, helping us push past boundaries that no longer serve.

Colors

Turn on the heat. Color is a great way to shift a space that is too yin to one that is just right, but chances are, if you are holding a lot of yin energy in your body, you will be fearful of including bright colors in your space. Start small. Put a bright red teapot on your stove. Buy a set of deep plum sheets. Float tangerine orange and Mediterranean blue candles in your bath.

Furnishings

Be firm. No slouchy couch for you. Opt for one with wooden arms and a firm seat. Use mirrors, glass, and polished stone. Be certain to replace hanging plants with plants that point upward and hang pictures higher than eye level. Remove items that sit directly on the floor, such as baskets, books, magazine racks, or knickknacks.

Lighting

Go natural. Bright lights can enhance your mood in addition to your walls. If at all possible, use natural light. Natural light includes the full spectrum of color vibrations for a balanced emotional and physical impact. Our favorite rooms are usually those that have natural light on two sides because the proportion of natural light to artificial light is 50 percent or more. If you do have a room with a single window, consider the possibility of putting in another window (it is less expensive than you think to have a wall made into a window). If you cannot work with the walls, add skylights.

When adding natural light is not possible, take off the window coverings, add a row of track lighting, and install lights under counters. Go for overhead lighting rather than lamps, use halogens that send light upward instead of downward pointing lamps.

Windows & floor treatments

Think open & clean. Fluffy and soft is not what you are after. Remove curtains or replace with wooden blinds. Opt for vertical blinds, rather than horizontal treatments. Allow marble, tile, and hardwood floors to lend you strength and provide the assurance of a stable foundation. Make certain surfaces are smooth and glossy to speed up chi flow and pull you out of an emotional mire.

Density & size

Lighten up. Too many furnishings can weigh you down, create stagnant chi, and make it hard to get moving. Make certain pathways between furniture items are at least three feet wide, preferably four. Use furnishings that are lighter in weight and smaller in stature, such as items made from wicker or bamboo. In the kitchen, clear off counters and streamline appliances.

18

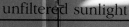

straight edges

bright colors

leather surfaces

unfiltered sunlight

hardwood floors

sparse furnishings

What do you need from your environment?

Your body and your environment are constantly exchanging energy. Your physical environment affects the energy in your body and the emotions and electromagnetic charge in your body leave their imprint on your environment. Once you have an idea of whether you carry more yin or yang in your body, you can work with this dance of energy to create more balance in your life. If you hold a lot of yin in your body, increase the amount of yang in your environment. If you hold too much yang, add yin energy in your home.

Let's say you are choosing flooring for a home office. Assume you have a naturally high energy level and are having a hard time focusing in the office. The house has an open floor plan with lots of windows and light-colored furnishings. If you choose hardwood flooring, shiny tile, or vinyl, it will speed up energy and make it even more difficult for you to concentrate. If you choose a thick textured carpet in a muted hue, it will slow down the energy in the room, help you anchor (ground) the energy in your body so that you can channel that energy into your work.

Note: This is not always a case of choosing what feels natural to you. If you tend to have a predominance of yin in your body, design choices that feel natural (in kin with your nature) will have a strong yin force as well. Although we often intuitively balance out a strong yin by bringing in more yang and vice versa, sometimes you need to consciously work with this balance. The more out of balance the body is, the less it will crave what it really needs. In this case, take inventory of how each item that you bring into your space shifts the yin/yang balance. Do not add too much too fast or you will begin to feel like you are living in a stranger's house.

Understanding the elements

Fire:
expansion &
transformation

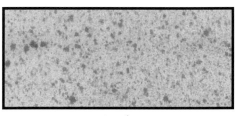

Earth:
grounding & support

Wood:
personal growth

When considering your space in terms of energy, the flow between yin and yang forces is a good place to start. You begin to view design choices according to how they move energy: whether it expands or contracts, moves higher or lower, speeds up or slows down. The five elements in feng shui explain how yin and yang manifest in five primary energy patterns. When you use the five elements to balance your environment, this balancing works inward and you feel it in your body. You might just notice that you are inclined to relax more in one room than another or that certain spaces invite you to stay longer than others.

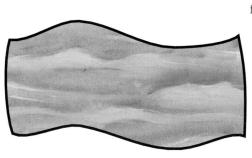

Water:
release & renewal

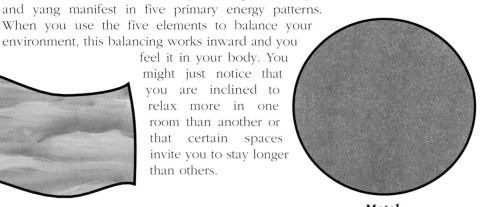

Metal:
mental power

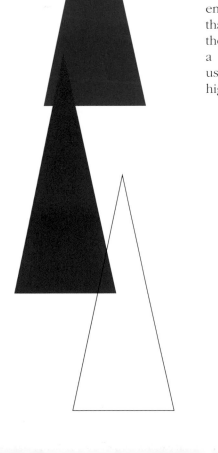

Fire: expansion & transformation

Fire is the power of transformation. Lots of fire energy in a home encourages lots of changes in the lives of those who live there. Fire energy helps you expand, open up to new ideas and ways of being. It gives you the push to share your gifts with the world.

Fire colors

You can increase the amount of fire energy in your home by the colors you choose. Although red and orange are traditionally associated with a fire vibration, any bright color will achieve the same energetic effect. What you are looking for is a certain dynamism, an active color that bounces light and energy.

The type of paint finish you choose also effects how much light energy is in the room. A semigloss will create a more reflective surface than a flat or a satin finish and will keep the light moving, increasing the energy in the room. High-gloss trim is a great way to add punch to a room. If your goal is to slow the energy down, however, consider using satin, eggshell, or flat finishes instead of semigloss, and avoid high-gloss trim.

Increase the amount of fire energy in your home through color, such as these bright yellow walls accented by the red standing clock. The triangular shapes throughout this room also increase fire energy.

Fire shapes & structures

Shapes and structures affect the energy of a room just as much as color. Shapes that generate fire energy are triangles (straight up or inverted), pyramids, diamonds, and sunbursts. These shapes send energy up and out and keep things moving.

Triangles represent the union of heaven, earth, and human. Triad energy is always volatile and fast moving. The straight lines and sharp angles keep energy speeding along and change is inevitable. This is a good shape to use if you want to shake things up or bring change to a certain area of your life.

If you are drawn to triangles in your decorating, there is a reason why that fast, changing energy feels good to you. Think about what it is in your life that you may want to change and consciously use triangles to represent that life aspect.

Pyramids represent eternal life and communion with the gods. Based on earth but directed towards heaven, a pyramid reminds us to honor our own divine nature and that, by honoring it, the mundane is transformed into the sacred.

Pyramids are more grounded and less volatile than triangles because of their solid base and three-dimensional quality. They will help you reach for something that you felt was beyond you or joyfully accept acknowledgment for the divine being that you are.

Diamonds are another way to bring energy into a room. Diamonds direct a downward-moving energy up and out. Known for their brilliance, they represent your ability to shine and radiate your life force out into the world.

Diamonds can be easily integrated into your design through tile work. Other ways to use diamonds include stained glass work, wallpaper, and windows. You can even transform a normal square window by adding a diamond stained-glass insert. Fiery colors in the stained glass will enhance the fire vibration even more.

Sunbursts shoot energy out in every direction. They symbolize the transformation that occurs every morning as the first rays of the sun shoot out over the tops of mountains, turning the stillness of night into the activity of day. Sunbursts also mark high noon, the sun in its full radiance. When you bring sunbursts into your home, you encourage recognition of your own radiance and the potential to transform any seemingly dark aspect of your life into light.

Fanning out floral arrangements at the top creates the expansive energy characteristic of fire.

24

To shift priorities to family and serenity, keep the television cabinet doors closed when not in use and use the fireplace often in season.

The diamond-shaped designs on these entertainment center doors keep energy moving in a vertical direction.

Design ideas for increasing fire

The lighter, brighter, and more reflective a room is, the more fire energy it holds. Paint walls semigloss instead of a satin finish, or paint trim a high gloss instead of a semigloss. Consider high-gloss picture frames instead of matte ones.

Increase the actual amount of lighting by adding spotlights, tea lights, lanterns, halogen lamps, or candles. Replace hanging plants with upward-shooting palms or yucca trees, and make certain they are planted in terra-cotta pots.

Pets are another way to increase fire vibration in your home. Even adding items that come from animals, such as feathers or leather, will increase fire.

Fireplace & television. There is a fundamental reason why homes with a fireplace sell faster than homes without. A fireplace echoes the days of the hearth, a sense of home, comfort, nurturing food, and good company.

Where a fireplace and a TV coexist, whichever object is more prominent will energetically and psychologically dominate the room. Shifting your relationship with your TV set, reducing its prominence by placing it behind closed doors, getting rid of a set, or moving it out of a prominent room, can reflect a shift in the prioritizing pattern of your life.

Cooking with fire. Fire energy burns away stagnation and returns the spirit. If you do not have a fireplace, use your stove. Notice how different it feels to use your stove instead of your microwave. Even if you are boiling water, lighting your stove (preferably a gas stove) generates an increase in personal chi, especially as it relates to overall health and the immune system.

Light on two sides. We require sunlight in order to survive—without it, our skin, mood, and overall health suffer. When people have a choice, they gravitate to rooms which have light on two sides, and leave the rooms which are lit only from one side unused and empty.

Natural light on only one side prevents chi from flowing smoothly from one side of the room to the other.

With natural light coming in on two sides of a room, the chi flow is balanced and draws energy across the room.

Earth: grounding & support

Earth energy is your grounding cord, your sense of safety, security, protection, and stability. It moves downward, holding things in place, making them stable and steady. Earth energy also moves slowly. It can manifest as dense, solid, heavy objects or as soft, comforting, nurturing objects. Either way, the effect is to become still, feel calm, and be at peace.

Earth energy reminds us that we live in a physical world with physical needs and to honor the physical body. Earth elements with a lot of density ground the body as well as the spirit and help you feel your body's messages. The result of really listening to the body is balance and improved health.

When you do support yourself physically by buying the right chair or couch, that supportive energy ripples out into other aspects of your life. You begin to notice where you are not psychologically or emotionally supported and you start to identify how you would like that support to be manifested. You will feel more empowered to ask for support from your spouse, boss, and children when you learn to support your physical body by doing something as simple as choosing the right chair. You are taking an action that affirms in your psyche and spirit that you are worthy of and ready to accept supportive energy in your life.

Earth colors

Earth colors are muted rather than bright, dark rather than light, and grayed rather than clear. Browns and yellows are traditionally associated with earth energy, but be careful that the yellow is not a clear, bright yellow.

Earth colors slow chi down and help you center your energy lower in your body.

Earth shapes & structures

Earth structures provide stability and comfort. When made from earth materials such as brick, adobe, straw, or stone, the earth vibration in the structure increases exponentially.

Horizontal shapes encourage cohesion and connection. This energy flow is not concerned with growth as much as it is concerned with integration. Every home has a lot of horizontal shapes and structures such as tabletops, desks, beds, shelves, and ledges. What you do with these surfaces determines how strong the earth vibration is.

For example, if you cover your table with a cloth, perhaps even a thick velvet cloth, you increase the table's holding properties. If you put a glass top on your table, you decrease the table's ability to hold and slow energy. Make your choices according to your needs.

Horizontal patterns hold energy, vertical patterns keep it moving. You can use horizontal patterns to slow down a fast vertical chi flow.

Squares and rectangles used in your home express a desire for right action and integrity. Your living space becomes the foundation from which this right action moves out into the world. Rectangles are a particular form of the square which can either ground energy (if the longer side is horizontal) or move energy (if the longer side is vertical). Horizontal rectangles create a strong earth vibration. Switching from a tall dresser to a side-by-side, exchanging portrait pictures (vertical) for landscapes (horizontal), and choosing wide (horizontal) windows instead of tall (vertical) ones will all increase the grounding in your home.

Squares in the picture frame, coffee table, and fireplace bring in earth energy.

30

Replacing plastic pots for terra-cotta pots draws in earth energy.

Design ideas for increasing earth

You can create an earth vibration by increasing comfort or stability. You want your family and guests to feel as if they are wrapped up in a cozy blanket in mom's kitchen. A little clutter can actually be a good thing here, especially if things are placed low to the ground. A basket here, a ceramic rabbit there, will draw energy closer to the earth and increase the downward pull of the space.

Remove transitional items such as futons, which are used as a couch one minute and a bed the next. A bed with a headboard and a regular couch will slow down change and increase the feeling in the room that life is stable, safe, and trustworthy.

To increase safety and stability in a room, add heavy furniture such as armoires, buffets, or cabinets.

The built-in oven and refrigerator add to the stability of this room. Using organic materials, such as the black granite in this countertop, also increases earth energy.

Walls. Thin walls made from sheetrock or drywall do not have the ability to hold energy as thick walls do; they lack density. Brick or adobe walls bring a more stable, grounded feel. You can create this grounding visually through faux-painting, rag-rolling, or layering paint. Whether you create the look of marble, brick, or aged stone, the paint gives depth and density to a flat wall. You can also create thick walls by building into or on the wall itself. Built-in furniture pieces such as window seats or bookshelves give your wall and your home the energy of permanence.

Ceilings. What's modern, exciting, and trendy does not always serve the soul, and this definitely applies to ceiling height. Vaulted, slanted, or high ceilings lift energy up and keep it moving. Low ceilings also have their place in the home, especially in bedrooms. Because they hold energy in and help people close down overactive receptors. They increase feelings of stability, permanence, and safety.

If all your ceilings are 10 feet or more in height, you can visually lower the ceiling by choosing the right lighting fixture. Lighting fixtures that hang lower draw the energy of the ceiling down and achieve the same effect as a low ceiling.

To add earth energy, consider adding one or more of the following built-in items:
▲ Garbage disposal
▲ Spice rack
▲ Desk
▲ Bookshelves
▲ Window seat
▲ Telephone ledge
▲ Bunk beds
▲ Breakfast bench
▲ Ironing board
▲ Garage shelving
▲ Tool bench

Wall faux finishes

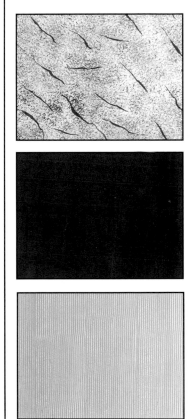

Metal: mental power

Metal energy is the energy of the mind. Like the mind, it has two primary aspects, the left-brained, intellectual aspect and the right-brained creative aspect. The left-brained aspect is dense, and its density serves as a magnet to draw scattered energies together to a physical center. It helps you focus and concentrate on intellectual tasks.

The right-brained aspect is dynamic, it pulls and pushes and spins, the natural result of many different energies coming together into a central location. Both forms pull energies together.

Metal colors

The feng shui colors for the left-brained metal vibration are white, silver, and gray. Many clients paint the interior of their houses white because they want a neutral feeling. This sharp edge can be helpful in some situations (an office for example) because it helps people focus on detailed tasks, such as computer programming or accounting. White walls in the more social rooms of your home, however, will not serve you well.

If you like the look of white walls, but do not want the sharp energy associated with them, opt for a creamy or rosy white. The creamy or rosy whites have an earth element as well as the metal and soften the overall effect. You can also leave three of the walls white but paint one wall a soft warm color. This one wall will balance the rest of the room and take away the sharp edge.

The right-brained aspect of metal is represented by rainbow colors. Bringing all seven rainbow rays into your home, especially into your creative studio, can be a powerful boost to creativity. Rainbow rays are also healing to the body.

White is anything but neutral it is intellectual energy; too much of it can make people sharp and sarcastic, similar to the sharp edge of an ax.

Metal shapes & structures

The circle is a yang form of metal energy. When metal melts, it forms droplets or circles. In a circle, energy is dynamic, constantly moving, pushing, pulling, and expanding. This is the natural result of combining energy flows. Although the circle shape spins energy outward, it also draws energies together. The wrapping motion of the circle draws the energy from one side of the circle to the other side. This means that circles pull separate strands of energy into a unified force, which it then spins outward.

In psychological terms, the circle shape represents the merging of individual consciousness with the collective. "To sit in circles is to array ourselves in a living mandala of community, offering the experience of being one voice in a collective awareness or effort. Cutting through the isolation and fear which is so characteristic of our culture, group practices ride on the interplay between our identities as individuals and as a collective, preparing us to be community members." (Vishu Magee, *Archetypal Design*, p. 109)

When we use the circle or the arc in our design, we bring communal energies into our living spaces.

When you sit in a living room where the furniture is shaped to form a circle, notice how it draws the energies of everyone sitting there into relationship with each other. Anything circular, such as the fireplace and center table in this photograph, can hold the sacred energy of community once you make the connection.

Increase metal outside by adding metal wind chimes, planters, a mailbox, or even a weather vane.

Metal items in round shapes spark the playful, yang aspect of the metal element.

Shiny metal like copper or brass, attracts more chi than dull metal.

Design ideas for increasing metal

Wind chimes and bells have long been used in many different meditation practices to call the mind back from its wanderings and return it to the present moment. They can be used to increase focus both inside and outside the house. Other metal objects such as tables, desks, shelves, or accessories can also boost the intellectual or creative energy in a room.

Even a wine cellar (typically a very earthy place) can have a strong metal element if you use metal and curves in the door.

The arc and the cut-away in this hallway are metal's more yin forms. They pull energy in towards a central point, condensing and focusing it. Yin metal energy increases concentration and intellectual focus. The strongest inward pull is at the inner angle or curve.

Water: release & renewal

Water energy has two aspects: still water and moving water. These vary greatly in their creation and their effect. Moving water (yang) moves energy from high to low, spreading out as it flows, equalizing the energy of all surrounding forces. It helps you release and let go of what no longer serves your best interests. It also represents the flow of money and abundance in your life.

Still water (yin) is a return to the womb. It settles, slows, and calms the energies surrounding it. The greater the stillness, the greater its ability to pull you out of a state of frenzied activity into quiet. It represents hibernation, germination, and gestation and is especially helpful when giving birth to some new aspect of yourself.

Water colors

The colors associated with water in traditional feng shui are black and dark blue. Black represents the energy of still water. Dark like the womb environment, it is the energy of universal consciousness from which individual consciousness is born.

Adding black to your space encourages you to develop inner wisdom and strengthen your connection with divine forces through an in-depth study of the self. It is also associated with new beginnings. A lot of black will send a strong message that you are not interested in social interactions.

When you move from black to deep blues, you engage the energy of moving water. It is the energy of moving water that directly influences career and the flow of money into your life. If you desire more movement and social interaction in your career, use deep blues rather than black.

Water energy allows you to relax and release anything you might have picked up during the day. Starting or ending your day in a water room will help you feel clean and free, both physically and emotionally.

Water shapes & structures

Still-water shapes. Any structure that recreates the energy of the womb will strengthen still-water energy. The still-water shape is the lake or the pond, where energy slowly moves inward and becomes still. Although a pond is more of an object than a shape, any object that holds the shape of a pond, or pictures of a pond, will increase still-water energy.

Moving-water shapes. Any shape that induces flow carries the energy of moving water. Traditionally drawn as rippling waves, terraces, or cascades, moving-water shapes direct energy sideways or downward.

Moving water directs energy downward.

An attic room with a low ceiling where the eaves come down around the person incorporates the still-water feature of a low roof. This space will feel more secure and protective than one with a vaulted ceiling.

To increase the energy of still water add an aquarium without a pump or a vase with flowers.

Design ideas for increasing water

Still water. To increase the energy of still water, lower your lights and add soft cushions, a vase full of water, or an aquarium with a low pump. On the outside of your house, add a birdbath, pool, or a pond. In still water features, it is important to make certain that the water does not stagnate. Ponds should be cleaned regularly and inside water should be changed daily.

The terraced steps leading down from the tub and the draped swag both increase the water element in this bathroom. The water is balanced by the strong wood energy in the tree outside the window and the upright wheat sheaves on both sides of the bath.

This outdoor pond incorporates water, wood (the greenery), and metal (the half-circle shape). Including at least three of the five elements in any feature promotes a balanced flow of chi.

Moving water. You can also increase downward movement by replacing horizontal blinds with drapes or by adding furniture pieces that slope, such as sleigh beds. Anything that hangs will increase water energy—mobiles, plants, jewelry, pots and pans, or even tools. Fish mobiles are a great traditional adjustment because both the fish and the downward movement of the mobile represent water.

Increase moving water with an indoor fountain as a symbol of abundance. If you place a frog next to the fountain, be certain he is leaping into the water, not away, or your abundance will also leave you.

Wood: personal growth

If you are interested in growth and creativity, think wood. Wood is the upward-moving energy that transforms seedlings into blooms and saplings into trees. Wood energy takes you beyond where you have been, and encourages you to be more, try more, and experience more. More focused than fire energy, wood energy is direct. It infuses your actions with purpose and meaning and promotes personal growth.

Wood energy is both the trunk of the tree, including the nurturing ability of the roots, and the branches that bend and move with the wind. It represents the union of earth (roots and trunk) and sky (branches and leaves) and the personal growth that comes from uniting those two forces.

Wood colors

Wood colors are clear and energizing, but not pastel. Traditional wood colors are green, which represents growth and healing, and purple, which represents abundance and expression. Avoid colors that have a lot of gray in them and appear muted or muddy. They slow growth.

Since the room has a low ceiling and ceiling beams, the vertical stripes painted on the wall lift the energy of the room. The tall wooden frames on the glass doors also generate the vertical flow of wood.

Wood shapes & structures

Wood shapes move energy in a vertical column, both securing roots and extending branches. Any shape or structure that shifts the flow of energy from horizontal to vertical strengthens wood.

Pillars. The triad of heaven, man, and earth is represented in the pillar. It is the force that connects the heavens with the earth, holding everything in between in a delicate balance. By incorporating pillars or columns in your home, you acknowledge your need for both heavenly guidance and earthly grounding. Pillars and columns should have rounded edges. If the edges are squared, you lose much of the vertical movement and create a problem with "poison arrows," the intense chi from a sharp edge.

Whether the pillar is simulated, as above, or is an actual pillar, at the right, this symbol unites earth energy with heaven energy for a peaceful balance.

Wood need not be heavy, such as this carved birdcage, which is especially auspicious since wood is related to the movement of air and wind.

Design ideas for increasing wood

Because wood energy connects us with the growth cycles of nature, any living plant will increase wood energy. Trees or plants that move upward, such as a ficus tree, are better choices than hanging plants. A hanging plant moves energy back down again.

When a rectangle is turned so the longest side is vertical, it generates a wood vibration. Therefore, to increase wood you would choose items that are opposite from an earth vibration. Instead of a side-by-side, you would choose a tall dresser. Rather than a vertical painting you would display a landscape.

Tall windows and cupboards as well as ladder-back chairs or grandfather clocks will also add vertical rectangles increasing wood. Items that are made of wood, such as cooking utensils, cabinets, hutches, or railings, all increase wood energy.

The upward-moving plant in the corner, the pillars outside vertical windows, and the tall wooden bookshelves all increase the wood element in this room.

Walls. If you do not have pillars or columns in your home, you still have wood energy. Your walls are a connecting force between heaven and earth. They draw the energy of the earth up towards the sky and bring it back down again. They connect the roof with the foundation and stabilize the vertical movement of energy through the house.

Increase wood energy in your home by emphasizing your walls. Wall treatments that include vertical patterns are powerful.

Using striped wallpaper or painting stripes generates wood energy. A faux painting of vines in this photograph directs the chi flow upward.

Vertical objects such as these bat rungs help move energy upward.

Working with the elements

Enhancing element energy

To enhance fire—add fire or wood elements (wood feeds fire and subdues earth). Design ideas: add tall chairs, pillars, palm trees or yucca trees, backlit plants, groupings of three, red or green candles, a carved wooden box, or lamps.

To enhance earth—add earth or fire elements (fire feeds earth and subdues metal). Design ideas: add terra-cotta pots, triple-wick yellow or red candles, large heavy items, brightly colored pillows, pottery, a rock garden, or warm cozy blankets.

To enhance metal—add metal or earth elements (earth feeds metal and subdues water). Design ideas: add low, wide furniture, a stone top on a metal table frame, long comfortable sofas, a brick pathway, metal chimes or bells.

To enhance water—add water or metal elements (metal feeds water and subdues wood). Design ideas: add rainbow windsocks, hanging plants, a copper fountain, a black or dark blue birdbath, a white vase, a curved path, or white tiles around the bath.

To enhance wood—add wood and water elements (water supports wood and subdues fire). Design ideas: add sloping or tall furniture pieces, a blue or green vase, flowing curtains, or vertical blinds.

Creating harmony & balance

Once you are familiar with the elements, there is a lot you can do to balance these elemental forces with colors, textures, composition, and shapes. This is not as daunting as it sounds, and incorporating it into your design will infuse your rooms with a sense of harmony and flow that is hard to pinpoint, yet is instantly noticeable.

Mapping elements

This exercise is helpful in getting a visual image of how balanced the elements are in your space.

1. Take a floor plan or draw a floor plan that shows walls, windows, and doors.
2. With colored pencils, color in a small area for each item that you can associate with a given element. For example, for the fireplace use red to mark a fire element, for the bathtub use dark blue to mark this water element.
3. Remember to mark items based on their shape or color as well as their composition. A black sofa is a water element, a brown chair is earth. A colorful floral arrangement that expands out at the top is a fire vibration and a pillar is wood.
4. For items that have more than a single element association, use some of each color when marking it. For example, if a pillar is white marble, it has an earth element (marble), a metal element (white), and wood (the pillar shape).
5. When you look at your element map, note the colors you have a lot and the colors of which you have very little. The goal is balance. Usually a strong presence of at least three of the five elements will provide a balanced environment. Use decor to bring in missing elements or to subdue any dominating elements.

Using cycles of the elements

Because of the different ways in which energy from each of the five elements move, certain element combinations will support, or enhance, a certain energy flow. Others will reduce, or subdue, those same energies. These two element cycles are commonly referred to as the constructive (enhancing) and destructive (subduing) cycles.

The constructive cycle

In feng shui, you can strengthen the energy of an element in two ways, you can add more of the element, or you can add more of the enhancing element. The enhancing element gives its energy to the element you are trying to strengthen. For example, water feeds and generates growth in trees. Therefore, to strengthen wood energy in your home, you could add more water energy.

▲ Fire generates ash (earth)
▲ Earth forms ore (metal)
▲ Metal condensation produces water
▲ Water nourishes wood
▲ Wood feeds fire

The bright (fire) colors in the pictures, the upright (wood) chairs, the horizontal (earth) table, the blue (water) dishes, the white (metal) blinds all work together to balance this room.

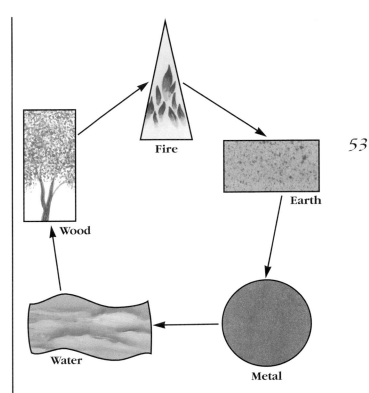

Wood

Fire

Earth

Water

Metal

To subdue fire—add water or earth elements. Water subdues fire and earth drains it.

To subdue earth—add wood or metal elements. Wood subdues earth and metal drains it.

To subdue metal—add fire or water elements. Fire subdues metal and water drains it.

To subdue water—add earth or wood elements. Earth subdues water and wood drains it.

To subdue wood—add metal or fire elements. Metal subdues wood and fire drains it.

If you know Chinese astrology, you can compare your home composition to your astrological composition and see whether your home is strengthening or weakening your personal chi. For example, if you were born with no fire elements in your chart, and your home has very few fire elements in it, it will not balance out the lack of fire in your body.

Too much of a good thing becomes destructive. For example, water extinguishes fire, or earth is washed away by water taking out necessary energy to stay balanced. You can use the energetic properties of different elements to subdue energies that might be too strong and out of balance with the rest of your home.

Balancing elements in your personal chi

Use the following descriptions to determine whether you have a strong or weak presence of any given element in your physical body.

Fire energy in the body

⇧ Too much fire energy can increase your feelings of anger and intense reactions. You might start to act rashly and not think things through adequately.

⇩ Not enough fire can leave you feeling cold, distant, unattached from life and other people. You might even find you swallow your anger rather than express it.

☯ Just the right amount of fire energy will keep you feeling motivated, alive, full of vitality, and connected to others. You will laugh easily, and feel the kind of joy that courses through your body.

Earth energy in the body

⇧ Too much earth energy causes smothering and stifling. You might feel stuck or worried that your loved ones will leave you. You can have a difficult time dealing with change and allowing abundance into your life.

⇩ Not enough earth energy creates a strong concern with survival needs. You might not feel safe or secure and might tend to look to others to provide your safety and grounding. You might tend to leave your body and hang out in your head more often.

☯ Just the right amount of earth energy provides a sense of safety and security. You feel centered, grounded, and respect your physical body.

Metal energy in the body

⇧ Too much metal energy can make energy sharp—enhancing feelings of sarcasm, feel nosy, self-righteous, or need to belittle others. With too much charge in the air, it is hard to relax, contributing to increasing stress.

⇩ Not enough metal can make you feel scattered and confused. Because metal increases the ability to concentrate and focus, it can also heighten difficulty in verbal communication.

☯ Just the right amount of metal energy allows for clear, well thought-out communication among family members. No single person dominates conversations, each speaks in turn. You are able to assert yourself, without being abrasive or rude.

Water energy in the body

⇧ Too much water energy creates a tendency to be overly emotional. There might be frequent crying and distress with no way to get the emotional body in harmony with the mental, physical, and spiritual body. Too much still water can result in depression and stagnation. Too much moving water can result in the feeling that life is moving too quickly and you cannot keep up.

⇩ Not enough water leaves you feeling drained and emotionless. Things do not flow; finances are strained; people are not as helpful; everything requires an enormous amount of effort. You might feel that things are scarce and that there is never enough.

☯ Just the right amount of water energy helps you feel abundant, at ease, and in harmony with the world. You can feel and express your emotions without getting overly emotional. Finances stabilize and there is a feeling of security.

Wood energy in the body

⇧ Too much wood energy makes for stubborn people. Like the oak tree, you might grow rigid and lose the flexibility of the bamboo. You tend to become focused on your goals, issues, and concerns, ignoring others.

⇩ Not enough wood creates a situation where things change randomly, without control or reason. There is no rootedness; you might start a project and then change to a new project without finishing the first.

☯ Just the right amount of wood energy is the essence of human kindness. You listen with empathy and truly desire to support others. You think things through carefully, are a good listener, and find others' opinions interesting rather than threatening.

▲ Fire melts metal
▲ Earth muddies water
▲ Metal chops wood
▲ Water drowns fire
▲ Wood breaks up earth

If you find that you have too much or too little of a given element, you can use the constructive and subduing cycles to bring your body back into balance. Remember that whatever energies are present in your body will have an effect on your body. Use your home to balance, support, and enhance your natural tendencies.

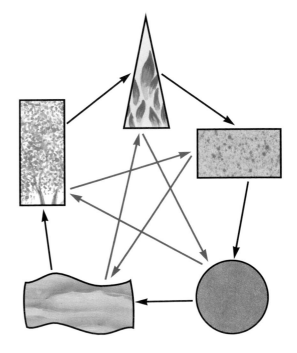

Ba gua fundamentals

When we align ourselves with the natural energy patterns of the universe, things flow more smoothly. When we do not, we place ourselves in resistance to the natural ways of things.

For thousands of years, Chinese have studied what happens to energy as it flows through a space. They discovered a predictable pattern between different physical locations in your home and different aspects of your life. They discovered that a certain part of your home relates directly to your personal abundance, another to career, and another to intimate relationships, for example. If a part of the home is missing, no energy flows to that aspect of life. On the other hand, if part of the home receives a lot of energy and attention, that area of life blossoms. This map of how energy flows through a physical space is called the ba gua. To bring harmony and balance into your life, align the energy in your home to the energetic patterns represented by the different sectors of the ba gua. To do this, you first need to map the ba gua onto your home so you know which areas of your home relate to which sectors.

Are you passionate about what you do for a living?

When you go to work, do you feel a sense of internal alignment, as if you were marshaling your energies together to focus them on the task in front of you? If not, which part of your body is in resistance?

Do you feel that something is preventing you from trying new things?

Do you feel that anything is possible for you to accomplish?

Do you feel like your life has purpose and that it gives you the opportunity to give your deepest gifts in the world?

Journey (career)

Journey is the beginning point of your life. It holds energy of the womb, winter, midnight, and gestation. Associated with the water element (represented in this room by the blue walls), this is the great mother from which all life springs. This energy is unbounded, infinite, open to the ends of consciousness and beyond. This sector is often referred to as the career sector because it also governs our beliefs about what we feel we can accomplish in the world.

How much time do you spend alone? Do you welcome it?

What kinds of things do you like to do alone?

Do you feel like there is enough time, money, or energy for your personal growth? If not, what are your energy drains?

When you get extra time or money, what do you spend it on? What needs are you trying to fill?

Do you feel that your boundaries are clearly defined? Do others often overstep?

Do you wear black or a combination of black and white often? If so, are strong boundaries important to you?

Self-knowledge (wisdom)

The energy pattern of Self-knowledge begins your emergence from the watery womb of Journey. Associated with the elements of earth and the mountain, this sector represents the process of individuation. This process involves setting clear boundaries and distinguishing your personal needs. As the mountain, you must learn to be still, centered, grounded, and feel your own strength. A single item, such as this chair, is a reminder to turn inward.

Do you have a tendency to hold on to things from the past that serve no purpose now?

Are you the storekeeper of the family heirlooms? If you are, the chi in this sector might be stagnant.

Do you display photographs of your family members? Are any members missing from your photograph collection?

Are there objects in your home that remind you of where you grew up? How do you feel about those objects?

Have you kept things that your parents gave you? What kind of energy do those objects hold?

When you look at things you created as a child, what empowered you to create them? What restrained you?

Family Heritage

The Family Heritage gua helps you learn about yourself within the context of a family. This gua holds the accumulated power of those who came before you and provides opportunities for your continued growth. The energy in this area holds the ambitions, dreams, desires, habits, and beliefs of parents, siblings, and ancestors. These energies are a part of your personal path, whether you acknowledge their influence or not. Associated with the wood element, they form the trunk of the tree from which you grow.

Are you happy with your financial situation? If not, where would you like it to be?

Do you make, but also spend a lot of money? Is there not enough to start with? Is there enough for what you want to do?

Are you passionate about what you do every day? Do you feel you can bring everything you are to it? Is your chosen career in alignment with your life's purpose?

In which areas of your life do you feel abundant? Do you have a lot of time? Do you enjoy the outdoors?

Do you have a rich social life and close friends? Rewarding relationships with children?

Do you have a naturally sunny disposition? A keen analytical mind? A sense for fashion? An ability to help others communicate?

Abundance (wealth)

As you align yourself with your life's purpose, you begin to feel more full of Abundance. Governed by the wind element and the color purple, this gua represents the opening up of energy that is always present. The wind brings us all we need. Our task is to open to its blessings. The energy of Abundance encourages us to be ourselves, to live our dreams, and give our gifts. This gua is associated with material wealth. Though money can facilitate the pursuit of dreams, focusing on money often prevents us from seeing other forms of abundance. By acknowledging the numerous manifestations of Abundance, our relationship with money often changes.

What would you like someone to recognize you for? How would they show you that they value you?

Is there anyone in your life who sees and appreciates what you do?

Do you feel visible?

Do you feel like you have something valuable to offer the world?

Do you feel comfortable dancing, yelling, or in other ways extending yourself in the company of others?

Fame (external recognition)

As you give your gifts joyfully, the world recognizes your efforts. This Fame sector is where you shine. It gives the world a way to say thank you and to affirm that what you are doing in your life is important. This recognition is not always in the form of awards. It can be cards from friends or drawings from children. Fame is governed by the fire element which is enhanced by the triangular-shaped window in this photograph and associated with symbols of transformation.

Are you in an intimate relationship? If so, are you happy in that relationship? Do you trust your partner and do you feel trustworthy?

How do you feel about your relationship with mother earth? Have you incorporated patterns into your life that support and nurture the earth, such as recycling, composting, minimal waste, and sustainable living.

Do you feel connected to something larger than yourself?

When you make a commitment to a person or a project, do you follow through with it? Do you allow yourself to receive help from others?

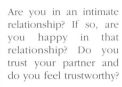

Intimate Relationships (commitment)

The Intimate Relationships gua encourages you to develop relationships of trust, openness, and mutual support. Ruled by the earth element, this area is dedicated to your connection with mother earth. It represents your ability to make a commitment to something greater than yourself (a career, a home, the earth, or another person) and your openness and willingness to allow others to support and nurture you.

Creative Offspring (children)

This gua is the playground of childhood. The natural result of receiving supportive and nurturing energy from an intimate other is a burst of creative energy. Sometimes this energy manifests the birth of children, sometimes in other creative projects. Whether you have children or not, everyone needs an area to play, explore, create, and destroy. Do not take yourself or the world too seriously. This sector is related to the metal element and pulls energy inward to a focal point. This inward movement generates the dynamics necessary to give birth to new creations, especially to create intellectual ideas.

Can you name five people who function as teachers, benefactors, or mentors in your life?

Are you currently functioning as a mentor to someone? How do you feel in that role?

How often do you extend yourself beyond your family?

What communities do you participate in? Business associations? Religious groups? Common interest groups? Men's or women's groups? Travel groups? If you were to open more fully to a sense of community, what type of people would you want to spend more time with?

Do you communicate with spirit guides? Activating this gua will encourage them to play a more active role in your life.

Helpful People (community)

The end of the life cycle is a time of sharing your gifts with a spouse, your children, and the entire community. Governed by the metal element, (all the circles in this photograph represent metal) this sector helps draw together the various parts of your life's story. This area of your home symbolizes your connection to a universal life force, your visible and invisible means of support, and your sense of community. This cosmic energy encourages you to call for aid from spiritual communities and heavenly beings, as well as physical neighbors. This gua is connected to travel.

Do you wake up feeling energetic and ready to start the day?

Do you get colds often or take longer than anticipated to heal?

Does life feel stressful and overwhelming?

Do your children have too little or too much energy?

Do you feel that your eating and exercise habits are in alignment with your spiritual goals?

Have you had any major health problems surface since you moved into your house?

Health

At the center of the home, the Health sector is where the energies of all the other sectors combine and balance. It should be open and free from walls, furniture, or hallways. The Health sector is governed by the earth element, representing your ability to nurture and support yourself. Your physical body lets you know when you are out of balance. This sector encourages you to be in your body, listen to its voice, and bring its needs into balance with the rest of your life.

The front door serves as the face of the house, the transition space between the chi of the environment and the chi of the house.

Applying the ba gua to your home

The ba gua is positioned according to "the mouth of chi." For an entire home, the mouth of chi is the architectural front door (where the house numbers are displayed), even if you use a side entrance, back entrance, or garage entrance more than you do the front door. Position the ba gua map so that the front door is either aligned with the Self-knowledge, Journey, or Helpful People sectors. To do this, go outside and stand facing the house. If your front door is on the left side of the house, then you enter your space through the Self-knowledge sector. If the front door is in the middle of the house, you enter into Journey. And if the front door is on the right side, you enter into Helpful People. These three guas form the front line of the ba gua (sometimes referred to as the Kan line). Assuming that the house is rectangular, the rear right corner will be Intimate Relationships, the rear middle gua is Fame, and the rear left gua is Abundance.

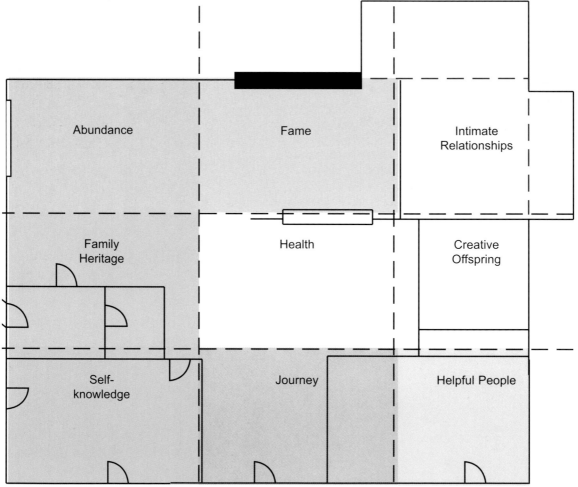

The ba gua lays over your floor plan as a template. The front door usually falls in either the Self-knowledge, Journey, or Helpful People sector.

Irregularly shaped houses create projections or enhancements, depending on the size of the extension. Typically, an imbalance in the structural design of the house corresponds with an imbalance in how the person experiences life.

Mapping irregularly shaped houses

Not every house is a perfect rectangle. Irregularly shaped houses create shifts in energy, pulling in more here and allocating less there. These shapes need not create missing sectors. Sometimes the shape creates a projection, or enhancement, of one sector, rather than a missing piece of another. In general, if the existing portion is at least half the width of the house, it has enough density to pull energy in on the other side of the house, thus creating a missing piece. If the existing portion is less than half, it projects energy outward, but does not create an inward pull. Therefore, the piece is projection and there is nothing missing.

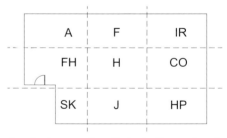

A missing sector distorts the natural pattern and cuts off the flow of energy to those life aspects associated with the missing sector.

A slanted wall reducing a sector requires special attention. Place an energizing object such as a plant or lamp in the corresponding sector of a room that relates to the missing sector.

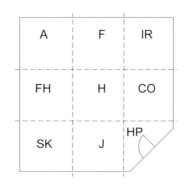

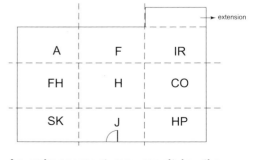

An enhancement may result in the abundance of energy in an area. More chi flows into the area associated with the related life aspect.

Floor plans

General features. This floor plan incorporates the best of two worlds, the closed doors and private spaces of the Victorian era with the wide open plains of the west. The blending of open spaces, where energy can flow, and smaller closed spaces, where energy can slow down and rest, help balance the yin and yang. Almost every room has natural light on two sides, increasing the overall chi flow and usability of the space.

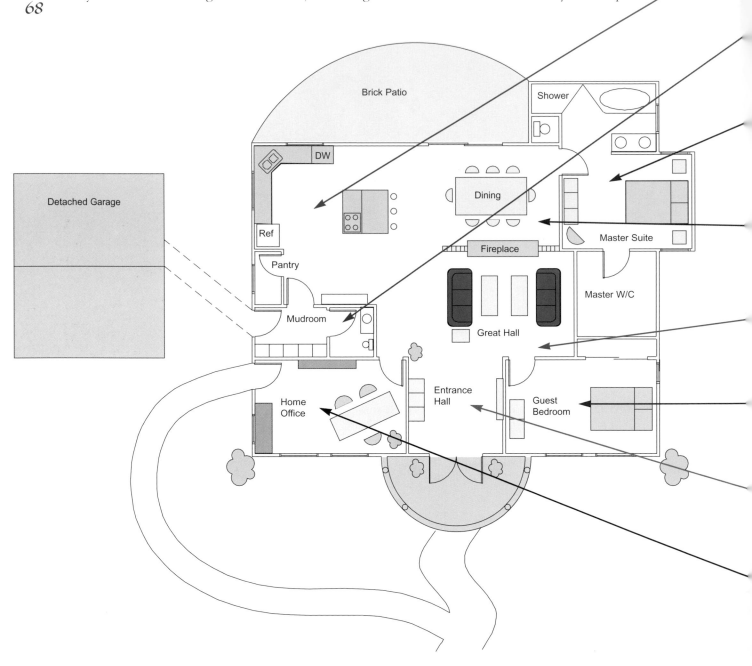

A good floor plan draws together many auspicious features and design details without creating problems for the inhabitants.

Kitchen. The kitchen provides an intimate association between the cook and family/guests. The island is two heights, a lower level for cooking and a higher level for bar seating. The wrap-around windows provide a restful view from the sink and create an active chi flow in the Abundance sector of the house. Fire and water elements have ample space in between.

Mudroom/guest bath. As the primary entrance into the house from the garage, the mudroom provides a transition space between the outside world and the private realm. Equipped with built-in storage cubbies and a bench for removing shoes and outdoor gear, this earthy room with tile floor and thick walls helps people decompress and release stress before coming fully into the house. The guest bath is placed next to this room to stabilize the downward flow of chi present in any bathroom. The two bathrooms on the main floor are totally separate from each other, which stabilizes chi flow throughout the house.

Master suite. The main-floor placement in the back half of the house make this master suite ideal, eliminating the need to navigate stairs while providing privacy and quiet. Located in the Intimate Relationships sector of the house, the bath area extends energy outside the outline of the rest of the house. This extension repeats on the right side of the room, providing an abundant energy flow for intimacy. Windows are positioned to the sides of the bed instead of directly behind the headboard maintaining a stable chi while sleeping. Moving other items, such as a TV or computer, out of the bedroom promotes deeper intimacy. The toilet area is visually separated from the rest of the space. The solid wall prevents views of the bedroom from the patio area. Plenty of closet space is provided to keep things well-organized and keep storage out of the bedroom.

Dining. The dining area enjoys the intimacy of the fireplace and the open freedom of the outdoor patio. The sliding doors to the patio let light in to the back half of the house, keeping chi from stagnating. Separate from the great hall because of the fireplace wall, this room can feel formal or casual, depending on the lighting. Located in the Fame area of the ba gua, the dining area is ideal for entertaining and socializing.

Great hall. This open center room balances the different energies that flow through the various ba gua sectors promoting good health. The glass block wall on both sides of the fireplace, between the great hall and the dining room, blocks energy from passing straight through from the front door out the back patio doors, while allowing natural light into the center of the house. The sidetable by the couch blocks the chi from the front door from hitting the seating area.

Guest bedroom. As a haven for Helpful People, the guest room is self-contained and placed in front of the midline of the house. The bed is placed with the headboard to a solid wall and windows are on the side. With a door opening onto the great room, guests are close to the center of the home without actually being in the middle. The closet provides a sound barrier and additional privacy for the master bedroom. A narrow vertical window to the side of the bed brings light into the other side of the room and keeps chi flowing smoothly. This room could be used as a child's bedroom.

Entrance hall. A winding path leads chi up to the welcoming double doors. The modern, curved porch, is anchored with wooden pillars to generate prominence and draw in chi from heaven (good luck chi.). The pillars do not to block the view of the door itself. A separate path encourages chi to flow around the side of the house to the home office. The entrance hall is wide and has a bench where guests can remove shoes. Plants ease the transition from the entrance hall into the living areas.

Home office. Placed in the front half of the house, this office is both accessible to visitors and still somewhat separate from the private areas of the home. Visitors enter the office from a side door. Located in the Journey and Self-knowledge area of the ba gua, this room encourages attention to work and inner wisdom. The desk is positioned to provide a view of both doors, with solid walls behind the chair. The windows are placed to the side, providing light and keeping energy moving. A small side window on the left balances out energy on both sides of the room.

Enhancing ba gua sectors

If you find that you have a section missing in your home, or that a sector does not receive as much energy as you would like it to, you can restore balance by directing energy to that area For the adjustments to be as effective as possible, follow the processes outlined for each adjustment below; but feel free to substitute adjustment items that resonate with your lifestyle, your experiences, and your cultural and personal symbolism.

General adjustments. Depending on your situation, you might need to adjust for a missing sector either outside or inside the house. If you are living in an apartment, for example, the missing sector might be your neighbor's living room. In that case, you will need to work from within your own living space.

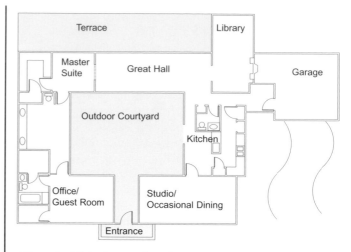

Plan A. This floor plan features an inner courtyard with a pond. This inner room is open to the elements and provides an intimate connection between the inhabitants and earth energy. However, a few adjustments are necessary to make this house harmonious with the ba gua.

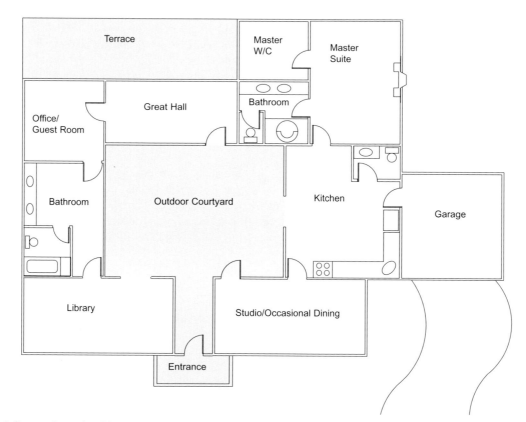

In the original floor plan, the library is positioned in the Intimate Relationships area and the bedroom is in Abundance. This adjusted floor plan has moved the bedroom to the Intimate Relationships area, the library into Self-knowledge, and the office into Abundance. Now the purpose and function of each room matches the energy of its location.

70

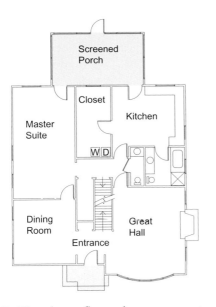

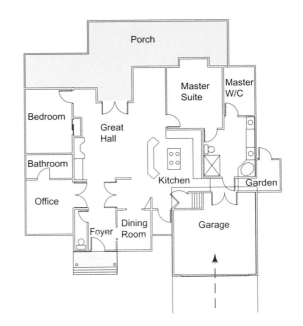

Plan B. The above floor plan opens onto a staircase, which creates a volatile fast-moving chi that flows right out the front door.

The adjusted floor plan (below) turns the staircase to prevent chi from draining and creates a spacious entry area. It reduces the size of the porch to avoid creating a missing area in the back. The location of the master bedroom and kitchen have been traded to match the ba gua sectors.

Plan C. The above floor plan is dominated by the garage. To reduce this prominence and balance energy throughout the home, the floor plan below makes several adjustments.

The entrance into the garage is turned to the side and a window is placed to face the front, making the garage look like living space. The home office and laundry areas are pushed out to fill in the outline of the house and bring more chi into the Journey and Self-knowledge areas. The bedroom and family areas are extended to eliminate missing Abundance and Fame areas. The master suite enhances energy in Intimate Relationships.

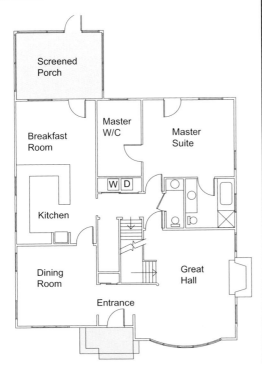

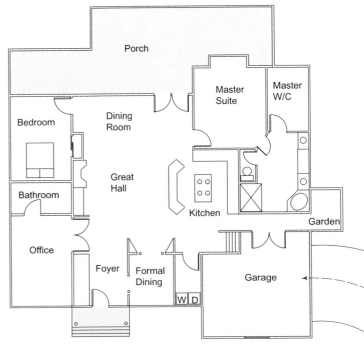

Organize each room by enhancing each gua with appropriate furniture and furnishings to balance and complement the room.

How does the ba gua apply to an individual room?

The ba gua is a metaphor (template) for understanding how energy flows. You can apply this template to an individual room, as well as to the entire house. As with the house, you determine the layout of the ba gua by the door into the room. If a room has more than one door, and if you use them equally, the door that lines up with the front door should be used.

The door into the room will line up with one of the bottom three sectors: Self-knowledge on the left, Journey in the middle, and Helpful People on the right. These are the three entry sectors. The other sectors always have the same positions relative to the entry sectors.

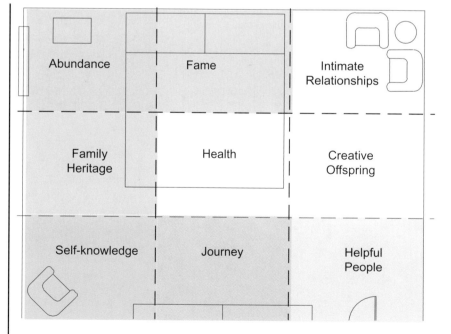

Chi flows into the Helpful People sector in this bedroom. Your bedroom door will either fall in the Self-knowledge, Journey, or Helpful People sectors of the room. The same rules apply to extensions and missing sectors.

The room-by-room guide

Journey (career)

Entrance. A Journey sector in your entrance affords you numerous opportunities to infuse new energy into your career. To announce to yourself and the universe that you are willing to show up and give your gifts, turn the porch lights on every evening, open the door to let fresh air in, and make certain the doorbell functions properly.

To stop backbiting or gossiping, hang gourds or bamboo on your door. The hollowed out spaces in the gourds and the bamboo trap negative energy and open up enough psychic space to allow you to respond rather than react when work gets challenging.

Bathroom. Although not common, it is possible to end up with a bathroom in your Journey sector. The water energy of the bathroom will work to enhance your career, keeping things moving and energy flowing there, as long as the energy that drains away is replenished.

Certain items hold symbolic significance. For instance, frogs are associated with abundance and prosperity.

If you want to change jobs, guide new opportunities to your door by displaying colorful flowers along the walk.

The wave pattern in the tile enhances the water element that governs the Journey sector.

Fix a round faceted crystal to the base of a hanging light fixture to refract the light and balance the chi.

74

Hallway/stairs. Stairs in Journey often find their way to the front door, funneling chi out of the house and away from those that live there. With a front door located in Journey, you might find that your job drains much of your life's energy. To slow and disperse the chi, place a large earthen pot with a live healthy plant in it at the base the stairs or at the side of the door.

Living room. A living room in Journey is great if you entertain as part of your job or if you are involved in a social occupation where you interact with people all day long. Think about the aspects of your job that you enjoy the most and represent them in your space. If you like writing, hang an intricate weaving on the wall to represent the process of bringing your ideas together in a balanced, creative way. If you enjoy a steady consistent income you can include a tortoise, the traditional symbol of longevity and consistency in career.

Kitchen. Not applicable.

If you love to be with people and have a career that requires some social savvy, add an entertaining piece such as a backlit liquor cabinet, a piano, or a sound system.

Dining room. The quality of the meals you eat reflects your relationship with work. If you tend to rush through meals, you will have the same tendency at work.

Storage area. If you feel like you have been put on perpetual hold, you can shift that by making a few changes in your storage area. Add a higher wattage bulb. Organize and prune it. Look at what you are storing in there. If what you are storing is mundane, do not expect your job to present exciting new challenges. To activate your career energy, place a mirror at the back of the closet or storage room directed towards the door.

If you honor yourself with healthy, balanced meals, you are more likely to find a healthy balance between home and work life.

Many career plans have been made and ideas hatched over dinner, so do not underestimate the power of a dining room in Journey. Whoever sits in the power position at the table (back to a solid wall with a view of all the doors) will enjoy greater power and esteem in the workplace.

To feel supported in your career, make certain you have a solid headboard behind you. The tall footboard in this room provides shelter from the chi of the door.

To attract a new job, place a spotlight on the outside of the garage door or leading up to the garage, illuminating your passage into a new career.

Bedroom. Bedrooms resonate with Journey energy. As a place of rest and rejuvenation, the bed prepares the way for a new beginning every day. If you feel constricted in your bedroom and have to maneuver around furniture, you will carry this constriction in your body each day as you go to work. If you have lots of open space in your bedroom, chances are that you will feel expansive when you get to work and draw new opportunities your way.

Garage. A garage is transitory, focused on coming and going. This instability in your Journey area can mean lots of starts and stops. To balance this, draw the garage into the living space by placing objects on the walls and by the door that one would normally expect to find inside. Children's drawings, potted plants, framed pictures, a TV or stereo, all extend your energy into the garage.

Self-knowledge

Entrance. The entrance through Self-knowledge encourages attention to an inner practice, something that strengthens inner resolve, peace, understanding, and wisdom.

Bathroom. Bathrooms in the Self-knowledge sector encourage one to turn inward and release what is no longer needed, including fears and perceived limitations. The act of bathing, itself, can be a meditation. Soak for ten minutes with bath salts to neutralize negativity in the body. Adding orange peels instead of salt, aids the release of sorrow and emotional pain. A single orchid on the vanity invites stillness.

If your Self-knowledge area is in a hallway, place an item associated with inner wisdom somewhere in the hallway, and an associated item in your sanctuary. Visualize energy passing between the two items, linking the energy of Self-knowledge with your sanctuary.

A bathroom can be used as a sanctuary. If your bathroom is located in Self-knowledge surround yourself with books and thought-provoking items.

Bring mountain energy into your kitchen by using granite, slate, baked-earth tiles, or other forms of rock and earth in flooring or countertop choices. Invest in the double-rounded finish for counters, so you are not slicing your aura every time you walk by.

For a Self-knowledge area in a kitchen, use stoneware pots to increase the association with earth and inner stability.

Hallway/stairs. The fast-moving energy of a hall and staircase is the opposite energy of Self-knowledge. Because this gua provides the grounding and stability for future growth, make certain all carpets are securely fastened down and banisters are secure.

Living room. With this combination, you have the most public room in the most private gua, a situation in which conflicts easily arise. You might feel too "available," as though your time belongs to everyone else. If you do, place a clock in the room next to your favorite seat to remind you that you, not someone else, decide how to spend your time.

Designate a favorite chair, one that soaks up your vibrations, so that it feels like coming home just to sit down in it. Indulge in a great set of earphones and turn stereo listening into a solitary pleasure. Discover the riches that await you inside.

Kitchen. Self-knowledge is the process of standing in your own strength, being your own mountain. Thick kitchen walls made of brick, straw, mud, or plaster not only give a room personality, they physically and psychically strengthen the person.

Dining room. Add a china cabinet to ground and stabilize the energy in the dining room. Because it is a heavy, stable piece of furniture, it holds a strong earth vibration. A china cabinet with an inside light represents inner illumination and wisdom. A buffet is another great way to add stabilizing earth energy.

If you have an inner practice, whether it is meditation, reading, yoga, or dancing, represent that practice on the door into your Self-knowledge area so you are physically reminded of it every time you enter the house.

If your dining room is large enough, consider placing an armchair with a lamp in a corner to extend the function of the space to relaxing as well as eating.

A single chair in the living room encourages solitary and reflection even if you never use it.

A beanbag encloses the aura and gives a secure, safe feeling. A dark-colored, cotton beanbag will help your children or friends release positive ions and stress better than light-colored vinyl.

Storage area. Store items here that instill a strong sense of self—a child's baseball mitt, a wedding gown, or a student ID card. A small closed space can be used as a sanctuary and assist in letting go of the external world.

Bedroom. The bedroom is a natural place to slow down and check in. Try using a reading chair or a bedside candle to encourage you to spend a few moments of mindfulness before crawling into bed. For children's bedrooms, use down comforters or lots of pillows to create a cocoon of safety.

Garage. Self-knowledge commonly ends up in the garage. Metaphorically, time for developing an inner practice is consumed with errands and driving long distances to day-care, school, or work.

If you like to read when you are alone, and Self-knowledge happens to be located in your garage, push some tools aside to make room for a few books.

Family Heritage

Entrance. Not applicable.

Bathroom. Downward-flowing energy is good for accessing past events and people. When we look down, our energy naturally moves into past time. To take advantage of this movement; add a photograph album of ancestors to the pile of books and magazines next to the toilet or place a photograph of your family tree on the wall.

Hallway/stairs. The hallway is a traditional place to display a coat of arms. If you do not have a coat of arms, display something sentimental. If you went on great camping trips in the mountains, hang a picture of your favorite mountain range. If you loved to sing together, convert a music stand into a hat rack, hang a trombone or trumpet on the wall, or frame a musical score. If you went golfing together, work a set of clubs into the decor.

A gallery of photographs or family treasures is a common way people remember their loved ones. The hallway and stairs area is the perfect place for such a display.

Consider meditating in the bathtub, especially if you want help or information concerning the past. In your decor, silver and nickel are the best choices for towel racks, lighting fixtures, and other accessories. Silver is associated with accessing past events and past lives.

Honor family members and ancestors by naming plants after them. As you nurture and care for the plants, you will find your family nurtures and supports you.

Living room. Parents are an important part of the Family Heritage gua. If you have unresolved issues with a parent, that issue will remain in your space in the form of stagnant chi and block growth and happiness in all areas of your life. Look for any large pieces of furniture that might block chi in the living room. Is your coffee table making it difficult to sit down or maneuver from one side of the room to another? Does your couch have its back to you when you walk in? Moving "block" furniture can open a way for resolving relationship issues.

Kitchen. Copper has long symbolized loving energy, so display your grandmother's copper molds. And if she passed on a sieve, sifter, or colander, displaying those will bring protection and comfort to your home. If you have a sharp corner that needs remedying in the kitchen, hang the sieve across from it. The holes in the sieve or colander can diffuse strong chi flows.

Invite your ancestors to be a part of your life by displaying their possessions. Share their stories with your friends and children.

Displaying family photographs and mementos in a storage area can create a get-away haven for reminiscing.

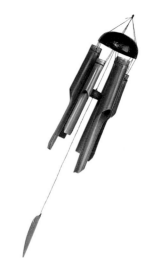

Bamboo lifts energy upward, creating a rising chi characteristic of the wood element.

Dining room. A dining room in Family Heritage is an energy vortex, a place where ancestors meet and interact with your present family. If you pull an empty chair up to the table, they might be coaxed to share their presence with you more often. For your table centerpiece, consider something with roots, stems, or branches in it. It could be dried branches from a nearby forest or wildflowers from your garden. When you look at the centerpiece, consider the many ways in which you are connected in this world and the prominent role family plays in forming who you are.

Storage area. Be conscious of what you are storing in this closet. Could you add your grandmother's wedding dress, photograph albums, your mother's dishes or bedding to it? If your entire Family Heritage sector is in a closet or storage area, there might be some family skeletons that need airing. If so, consider bringing your family energy out in other areas of the house. Look to see if there is a pattern with family energy in individual room ba guas. If you find that the Family Heritage sector shows up in a dormant or missing way in more than one section, use activators to get the chi flowing to that part of your life again. You can activate with lights, sound, movement (fans, fountains, wind chimes), or something alive (plants, pets).

Displaying loved ones photographs connects families together, whether living or deceased.

Ancestral heirlooms and collectibles in the bedroom create a bond between generations.

Displaying possessions from older family members keeps their presence with you when they are gone.

Bedroom. If you would like visitations from family members or ancestors in your dreams, include pictures of them in your bedroom. Add wood, plants, or upward-moving objects, such as bed posts, to support wood vibration in this gua.

Garage. This placement will keep your family origin and ancestors somewhat removed from your nuclear family because their energy is physically separate. Also, when Family Heritage is situated in the garage, you can anticipate more visits from or to family members. To ensure that the visits result in harmonious relationships, place a ba gua mirror (an eight-sided mirror that represents balance and harmony) in the Family Heritage area of the garage.

Abundance (wealth)

Entrance. Not applicable.

Bathroom. Abundance in the bathroom requires adjusting. Energy attaches itself to whatever has the most density and the strong downward flow of water in a bathroom carries the energy down and away from the house. Prevent energy from the rest of the house from coming into the bathroom by hanging a ba gua (eight-sided) mirror on the outside of the bathroom door.

Hallway/stairs. Since hallways and stairs funnel chi through quickly, the natural result of this placement is money that goes out as quickly as it comes in. If the stairwell is not visible to guests, funnel energy up by painting an upward-moving arrow on the wall.

In the hallway, slow things down so that you have time to enjoy the benefits of your hard-earned income. Whatever is at the end of the hall should be absorbent, yin, dark, and sturdy.

This three-legged toad is associated with abundance. The ancient myth claims that on the eve of the full moon the three-legged toad would appear outside the home of someone about to receive news of good fortune. To draw good fortune to your home, place a three-legged toad in your Abundance sector.

In stairwells, it is helpful to place pictures or wall fixtures in a horizontal line to stabilize the downward-moving chi that is naturally created in a stairwell. If you angle pictures down the stairs, it increases the downward tendency and can create chi that moves so quickly that it does not feel comfortable.

In the bathroom, remove anything that hangs down: plants, towels, and shower curtains. Add standing plants to move energy upward. (Jade plants represent abundance because their leaves are shaped like coins and move upward.)

Place the hand of Buddha in the living room to draw upon the energy of this tradition.

Living room. Since we tend to place our most opulent possessions in our living rooms, this placement works well for Abundance. The only problem is that people sometimes forget to spend time in their living rooms. If the room does not receive any active chi, it will stagnate and so will your cash flow. Make certain this room gets daily attention. If you are not into dusting or vacuuming, open the windows or turn on the stereo. Fill your living room with items that make you feel fully alive.

Kitchen. A kitchen can inspire a feeling of plenty. Stay away from stark black-and-white or stainless steel kitchens in this case. While they might feel clean, they will not promote Abundance.

If you do not cook much in your kitchen, you will need to keep chi active in other ways. You might want to add a ceiling fan (but not above the cook).

Decorative living room storage cabinets in the Abundance area are perfect for displaying favorite treasures, as well as providing easy access storage for prized possessions.

Your health is an important Abundance attribute. Keep healthy foods on hand and continue to eat well.

Dining room. If you want more in your life than an abundance of food, watch carefully what you place in the center of the table. Fill a bowl with an abundance of flower blossoms, leaves, or fruit.

Storage area. If you want to hang on to and save your money, this can be a good place for your Abundance sector. But because this area of the house tends to be more yin than most other areas, it will have a slow chi flow. If raises are not coming your way as quickly as you would like, you might want to move things a bit, add a brighter wattage bulb or paint the inside purple.

Place an abundance of fruit in the basket or lots of potatoes in the bin to keep your Abundance area looking full and prosperous.

Nine I-ching coins in a box under your bed can initiate a positive shift in your finances.

Bedroom. There are numerous feng shui rituals that involve money in the bedroom. Most of these involve physically placing money within range of your auric field while you are sleeping. All these cures link your personal chi to the manifestation of physical money. When it is physically present, you will think about it more, send energy to that part of your life, and draw more energy in the form of money into your life. Be careful though. If your Abundance energy is directed solely towards making money, you might make a lot of money but not experience Abundance in other significant areas of your life.

Garage. When your garage is in Abundance, pay attention to your car. Your car is a reflection of you. Keep it clean and taken care of, then carry this feeling into your financial affairs. If you travel a lot for your job, consider placing a red envelope with a $100 bill somewhere in your car to show your desire for abundance in your career.

The pillars of this four-poster bed are great for a bedroom located in the Abundance area of the house.

Fame (external recognition)

Entrance. Not applicable.

Bathroom. Fame and recognition energy resonates with fire. Therefore, a bathroom in Fame is difficult because the downward-moving water energy of the bathroom conflicts with the upward, expansive energy of fire. Remedy this by incorporating upward-moving patterns. Tile borders that create a horizontal line halfway up the wall help hold the energy in the space and keep it from moving downward. Avoid hanging plants, especially over the toilet, and choose a shower curtain with vibrant colors and a design that moves the eye upward. Place a brightly colored rug outside the bathtub and be certain lighting fixtures direct light upwards.

Use bright colors and a variety of textures and patterns to keep Fame alive.

This bathroom is a strong expression of the owner's personality, which encourages her to be more fully herself whenever she enters the room.

A great way to bring drama to a room is to add crown moldings. This brings everyone's eye up high, which raises their chi, enhances your reputation, and leaves everyone feeling better.

Hallway/stairs. Neither people nor energy spend much time in hallways and stairs. We tend to hurry through to another destination. Chi also hurries through, creating a volatile space where things can change fast. To stabilize, place a large object at the end of the hall, such as an earthen pot or a chair. Texturize the walls or use wallpaper with a lot of texture. Add a runner to the stairs or place a long thick rug in the hall.

To increase a fire vibration, make certain the hall and stairs are well lighted and that the ceiling is lighter than the walls. Avoid hanging light fixtures. Add bright colors in rugs, flowers, and pictures. If your hall is neutral in color, consider painting the door or wall at the end in a vibrant color. If you do not want to paint it red, go two shades lighter or deeper than the rest of the walls.

To provide a good view of the area behind you without cutting people up into pieces, use a convex mirror. The curve of the mirror provides a wide angle view of everything behind you without taking up a lot of space and becoming conspicuous.

If you have a fireplace in Fame, make certain it is never dormant. During summer months, fill the fireplace with flowers, lights, white birch logs, or something bright to bring energy to the space.

Living room. For a reputation boost, paint one wall red, the other three walls taupe, and the trim a high-gloss white.

Kitchen. The kitchen is a wonderful location for Fame. Your prime real estate here is the refrigerator door. Do not be shy displaying all the great things that everyone in the house is doing. Children's drawings, notices of school plays, flyers for workshops, newspaper clippings, or thank-you notes from friends. Copper is key in creating a Fame vibration in the kitchen. As the most radiant metal, copper activates dormant energies surrounding it.

Dining room. Whatever gets displayed in the middle of your dining room table should tell a story about you, your passions, what you love in life. If you love gardening, create an herb garden in the center of your table. Because Fame is the energy of transformation, butterflies, dragonflies, or a phoenix on the door are wonderful to display in this sector.

When choosing plants, consider palms and succulents. They bring in more solar power. Palms that fan out are symbolic of the radiant energy force of Fame and recognition.

Storage area. It is hard to be dramatic about storage, but you can still influence energy. Use shelves to take advantage of vertical space and move energy upward in the room.

Bedroom. It is difficult to create a Fame atmosphere here. When we feel valued and recognized, we feel energized and passionately alive—not a state that is conducive to sleep. Find an area of the bedroom that is separate from where you sleep and dedicate that area to an awareness and appreciation of your own expansiveness.

Garage. If you can open up a window in your garage, adding natural light is an excellent way to enhance Fame energy. Make certain your overhead light is working and that storage is kept to a minimum. Get artistic in your garage—anything that actually goes through a transformation—on the walls.

Candles increase illumination and Fame energy in any room.

To keep life s excitement use colorful, imaginative containers for storage.

Fame is associated with physical beauty. Find an area of your bedroom to dedicate to the things you find beautiful.

Intimate Relationships

Entrance. Not applicable.

Bathroom. A bathroom has a strong downward energy, correlating with a water vibration. If you tend to get emotional often, be aware that water controls the emotional body, too much water in Intimate Relationships can manifest in tears and depression.

If you live alone, make some room for another person. Buy a second toothbrush and pillow or include objects that represent the type of person you want to meet.

A bathroom is great for intimacy because flowing water deepens the emotional connection. If things get too emotional, however, stabilize the flow of water with earth elements.

Open staircases (above) in Intimate Relationships indicate volatile, quickly changing relationships. Stabilize open staircases by filling in risers and adding rugs, as in the photograph below.

Hallway/stairs. Stairs and hallways tend to speed up chi flow, ushering in change, movement, and shifts. If you want things to change, great. But if you want to stabilize the relationship, place a small convex mirror at the bottom of the stairs directing energy back up or hang a round faceted crystal from the light fixture at the bottom to disperse the strong chi flow. If you have an alcove in the hallway, place a statue of two lovers there. (This can be as symbolic as you need it to be, depending on where your hallway is located.) If you like wallpaper, place a wide horizontal border halfway up the wall in the hallway to stabilize chi.

Living room. Be careful not to invite the public into your intimate space. This includes not sharing things about your intimate life with friends that they do not need to know. To draw the energy of intimacy into a more private space, such as your bedroom, link the areas by placing a rose quartz crystal in the living room and another one in the bedroom. Make certain that the one in the bedroom is larger.

If your Intimate Relationships area falls in the living room, use artwork to remind you of your relationship with your loved one.

Kitchen. The danger of having a kitchen in Intimate Relationships is that you will nurture and support yourself with food rather than with people. To avoid this, keep the people in your life physically present in the kitchen by displaying photographs on the refrigerator.

Food is intimate, so when you are in the kitchen, make it a time to talk about intimate topics. Copper has a long tradition of opening the heart, so use copper pots or display copper molds. To spice up a relationship, display your cooking spices, especially cinnamon and cayenne pepper. Stuff a pot holder with spices, add them to your cooking, simmer potpourri. The more you see, use, and smell them, the more yang chi will flow through your body and love life. To symbolize the union of your energies with your partner's, tie two dish rags or hand towels together and place them in the bottom of a kitchen drawer.

Dining room. A dining room in Intimate Relationships can help ground your relationship in the physical world. This area of the home relates to the lower chakras and will balance out an overly intellectual relationship. Because a dining room is a public room, have fun with covert expressions of passion.

Storage area. This placement signifies a dormant period in your relationship energy. Placing a large mirror on the inside of the storage room directed at the door can keep energy active. Even if it is your personal closet, make certain there is at least one item that represents your partner.

Keep Intimate Relationships in mind even in a busy kitchen by keeping a bottle of massage oil in with your cooking oils. (Make certain the children do not mix the two up when it is their turn to cook.)

A bowl of pears in the kitchen or dining room can represent your pairing with your partner without anyone being the wiser.

Beware of placing packing boxes in the Intimate Relationships sector as they may encourage your partner to think about moving on.

96

Uncut crystals in the bedroom are a constant reminder of mother earth and provide stability and support.

Bedroom. This is a powerful combination of energies. If you are ready to attract a new relationship, hang a man's suit (or if you are a man, hang a woman's dress) in your closet. Make certain the clothes fit your ideal partner's size and style. Get rid of anything that is filling in for a relationship right now, such as stacks of magazines or bedside romances. Take out the time-consuming computer and TV that tempts with 24-hour distractions.

Garage. The risk here is that you will see each other only in passing. Life is busy and you each have your own agendas, schedules, places to go, and things to do. To adjust for this tendency, place items in a prominent position that represent activities you love to do together. Avoid placing things in prominent view that only one of you enjoys, especially if it is a source of contention.

If you love to ski together, place your skis where you will see them every time you get out of your car and enter the house. If you love to travel together, place something on the garage wall that you found on your travels.

Creative Offspring

Entrance. Not applicable.

Bathroom. Metal gives its energy to water so a bathroom here can drain energy from your creative storehouse. By adding earth you will strengthen your creativity. Add earth by using yellow or brown in your decor, bringing in terra-cotta planters, placing small stones along your window sill, or adding a bath pillow to your tub. With tile you can create a strong horizontal line around the bathtub, shower, or halfway up the wall. A horizontal line will strengthen the earth energy in the space.

Hallway/stairs. A picture gallery in the hallway does not have to consist of your creations as long as it inspires you to create. Use spotlights to energetically enhance your favorites. If you have a window, take advantage of it by placing flat leaded crystals in it or by hanging a radiometer to catch the light. The staircase can also display your creative gifts. Drape, twirl, or wrap tassels, lights, leaves, plastic fish, or whatever feels fun and playful to you.

Bring creativity into a hallway by painting a playful scene on a hallway door.

The leaf motif in the wall hangings and floor unite this hallway with the fall energy associated with Creative Offspring.

Set aside an area in the kitchen where crayons or chalk can be used for creative expression.

Living room. No matter how formal a space is, you can always add an element of fun and creativity. Find some way to represent your favorite creative outlet. Move beyond displays and show your playful side with furnishings. Remove the couch and throw a pile of oversized pillows on the floor. Place an antique door on a metal frame for a coffee table. Turn a walking stick or a trombone into a standing lamp. Paint a mural on your wall or around a doorway. Paint each of your four walls a different color. (This is much nicer to live with than it may sound.)

Kitchen. What better place to offer up your creative gifts, that is, unless you do not care for cooking. Regardless, choose a goblet to serve as your chalice and place it in full view to remind you that your creative gifts are many. With a white kitchen, throw a multicolored rug on the floor. Use all four burners on your stove, even if it is only to boil water. Use your refrigerator to display magnetized word art and play poet.

Make a formal living room more inviting and relaxing by displaying games and fun activities. Make an effort to actually play these games with family and guests.

Let a child fill his/her room with mementos and items representing things he/she enjoys doing. Photographs of friends and happy times are also appropriate.

To add metal in the dining room, consider a metal light fixture, lanterns on the buffet, or metal drapery rods.

The metal base and the playful colors of the marbles make this fountain a great placement in a Creative Offspring sector.

Dining room. A lot more than eating can happen at a table. If you love to write letters, do it at the table. A well-crafted letter is itself an art form. Try out different tablecloths and see how they change the energy of the room. Although Creative Offspring is governed by the metal element, avoid metal/glass table combinations. Metal next to glass creates a precarious and volatile energy that is not helpful to human beings. Metal tables and chairs are rarely comfortable and are best used outdoors where the sun can warm and soften them.

Storage area. You may store something fun in storage, but be certain to bring your playthings out once in a while. If your creativity closet is full of boring things, hang something whimsical and playful from the ceiling. Write on your boxes in multicolored magic markers.

Dreams are some of our best creations. Keep a dream journal next to your bed to help you remember them. Journaling unleashes the creative spirit and moves us through our creative blocks.

Bedroom. If Creative Offspring falls in a child's bedroom, set up play stations that are appropriate for the child's age. Choose toys that inspire creativity and can be torn down and rebuilt a hundred different ways. Make certain that this area gets fresh air often, at least twice a week.

Garage. Convert an area of the garage into a workshop. If gardening is your art, this is the place to display the tools of your trade. A garage also provides large walls perfect for painting a mural.

This hand-painted bedroom wall is a beautiful blend of creativity and playfulness.

Helpful People

Entrance. An entrance into Helpful People extends you beyond yourself, your relationship with a partner, and your family unit, into your community. Define the communities in which you want to actively participate and "call them" into your space. Calling in a community is much like creating a relationship with a spiritual guide. You place a physical object in the space to represent the entire community.

Bathroom. In bathrooms, we let go of what we no longer need and fill up with healing light. First make certain nothing is hanging over your head. No shelves or plants or even bathrobe hooks. If you have a window in the bathroom, a flat leaded crystal against the pane can bring in rainbow light. It will help balance your auric field and contribute to the healing rejuvenating vibration of the bathroom. Hanging a radiometer in the bathroom is also great for bringing in light energy to aid in healing. Work to include groupings of three or more.

Place three or more towels on your rack, three or more flowers in a vase, or three or more candles in the tub to promote community.

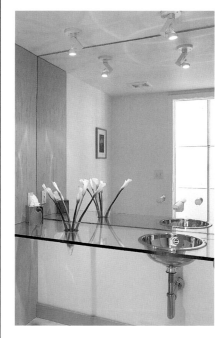

If you participate in a spiritual community of heavenly messengers and beings, surround yourself with angels to watch over you.

Bring music into the living room to enhance communal relations.

Hallway/stairs. The fast-moving energy of a hallway can bring a lot of change, fast, into your Helpful People sector. If things are moving too fast, slow it down with rugs, potted plants, or a heavy object. To enhance community interactions, think in groups. Place three or more candles on a table.

Living room. Since Helpful People is related to travel, it is a great place to display items that you brought back from your journeys. Those items hold the energy of the place where you bought them and they can call your energy there again. Use this sector to draw a trip to you. If you want to go to Africa, for example, place African masks or musical instruments in your living room.

Show your abundant travels in an exciting way, such as these tiles collected from around the world.

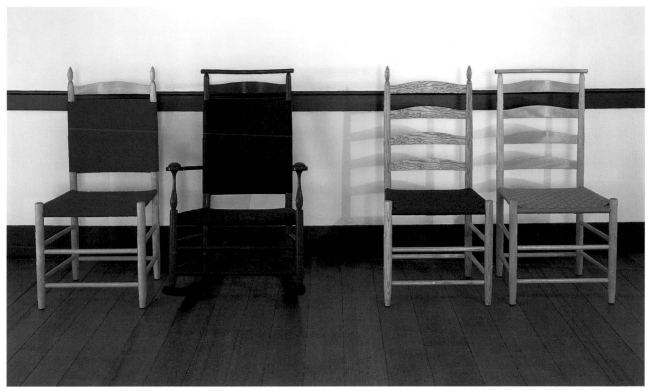

Mixing woods or styles in your dining set are additional ways to appreciate divers energies. Use chairs from different time periods or paint each chair a different color.

Kitchen. Everyone loves to gather in a kitchen; give them a place to sit. Ring a bell or wind chime every day to welcome in helpful energies. Group spices or countertop items together to remind yourself that you are supported in your efforts. Make the refrigerator a community bulletin board and display notices of events that you would like to attend or support in spirit. If you have a garden and reap a fall harvest, dedicate a sharing basket.

Dining room. Embracing community is embracing diversity. You can create diversity around your dining table by placing a multicolored rug underneath it. Place a bowl full of fruit, leaves, or blossoms on the table. The round shape of the bowl represents the circle of community.

Storage area. This area could create stagnation in your social life. If you have not made new friends for a long time, or have not been able to "get out" and participate, activate this space by painting an angel on the wall or by stacking your boxes in groupings of three or more. Store items that you received from friends. Hang something circular such as copper spirals.

If you love travel, use a trunk as part of your living room furnishings and display your treasures from various trips.

Use the door from the garage to the house as a portal that readies you for a return to your inner sanctuary. Sanctify that place as a portal by painting the door jamb gold or white and hang a small crystal from the top of the jamb.

The presence of angels in the bedroom invites protection from unseen beings.

Enhance your connection to other lifetimes and relationships by displaying silver elements in your bedroom.

Bedroom. Dreams and dream-time visitors can become an important component of your support system. The color and element silver symbolizes a connection to other realms and other lifetimes. You can add silver to your bedroom decor through a silver sheen in your paint color, silver items on your dresser, a strip of silver on a picture frame, or silver jewelry. If your bed is made of metal, expect to do more dream-state traveling.

Garage. Since it is related to travel, a garage can be a good placement for your Helpful People sector. Plaster travel posters on the walls or place an object in your car that relates to your next trip. The state of your car is directly related to the energetic state of your Helpful People sector. If the garage is clean and well organized, you can expect things to flow better. The right people tend to appear at the right time, connections are made naturally and easily, and you are aware of opportunities in which you could be helpful to another.

Health

Entrance. Not applicable.

Bathroom. A bathroom in the middle of your home requires adjusting. As water flows down the drain vital chi flows away with it. Allow energy to flow back into the bathroom by placing large mirrors and upward sconce lighting above the sink. The lights move energy upward and the mirrors magnify the upward movement. Be certain mirrors are not hung so low that they reflect the water pouring out of the faucet. High mirrors lift your personal chi and expand the energy field around the top of the head. You should be able to see six inches above your head in any mirror.

Hallway/stairs. One of the most problematic placements is when Health is located in a hallway or staircase. When the Health sector is blocked with a hallway wall or an enclosed staircase, energies cannot flow from one side of the house to the other. This blocked energy pattern tends to repeat itself in the body. Place a picture in the room that has depth to it to create an energy passageway.

Carpet stairs and make certain railings are securely fastened. Place a round faceted crystal at the top and the bottom. Open doors and windows to allow fresh air to pass through regularly.

Avoid mirrors with splits or two mirrors that meet in a corner. Both situations create a disturbing split image of the person looking in the mirror.

Place a large mirror in the room that shares a wall with the hall or stairs to create an energetic passageway between the hall or stairs and the room.

What you choose as a centerpiece represents the state of your health so choose carefully. If you have flowers, make certain they stay fresh. If you have a bowl of fruit, make certain the fruit is ripe but not mushy.

Living room. This room typically works well because it has large open spaces. The most important feature of the Health sector is that it stays as open and free of clutter and furniture as possible. Avoid placing large pieces of furniture in the middle of the room and keep the amount of furniture to a minimum. Hang mirrors to increase the amount of space you can see from the living room. The more you extend your visual command of a space, the more you extend your energy. To further enhance Health, consider creating half-walls or opening up normal-sized doorways into larger passageways.

Kitchen. There are many varying traditions surrounding stoves in the Health sector. Some Chinese traditions view this as potentially harmful to the heart. Native American traditions view the stove as representative of all life force and the central placement as being ideal. Our cultural associations affect how our bodies respond to this situation. In any situation, you can add earth elements to stabilize this area.

Use open wicker furniture to keep energy moving in a Health area.

If you have a choice, opt for an oval table instead of a square or rectangular one. Rounded edges will continue to move chi around the table and through the space, whereas square shapes will hold it still. If you have candles on your table, light them at least once a week.

Dining room. This open space works well for a Health sector. However, you usually have to place the table in the middle of the room. Adorn the table with a centerpiece which brings well-being.

Storage area. Since storage areas are typically small and closed in, this is not a good placement for your Health sector. Place a mirror on all four sides of the storage room or closet. This creates a vortex and allows energy to pass right through the closet. Invest in stacking solutions that allow you to create space inbetween layers of boxes. Place items on shelves instead of on the floor and keep things moving vertically as much as horizontally.

Keep your storage items organized and try to open up the space as much as possible.

Keep the bed off the floor, even if it is only a few inches and make certain you do not turn the space under the bed into an extra storage closet.

Bedroom. Watch out for that big heavy bed in the Health sector. Since the Health area requires open spaces to balance out and harmonize energies from all the other guas, a large bed can block the flow of energy and cause stagnation in the body. Keep under the bed free—chi needs to flow smoothly and freely under your body as well as above it for optimal health.

Garage. Not applicable.

Use lighter furniture to ensure chi can flow smoothly and freely around the room.

Where do I put it?

There is nothing more significant in feng shui than how something is arranged. The arrangement, as much as the individual items, determines how your environment affects you. Through arrangement alone you can slow chi down, speed it up, concentrate it in certain areas, smooth it out in others.

Most feng shui is based on individual objectives, but there are a few things that are best to avoid no matter your objectives. It is important to note that the dynamics created by certain furniture placements are not "bad" in the typical meaning of that word. Energy currents that energize and stimulate a cat will kill a bird and some chi flows are too intense or too fast to be helpful to the human body. The suggestions in this chapter will help you avoid placements that may undermine the immune system or disturb the psyche.

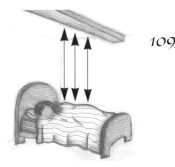

When you sleep under a beam, your body is exposed to the beam's intense energy when it is trying to relax.

Ceiling beams

A beam protruding out of a ceiling disrupts the flow of energy across the ceiling. Because beams are made from dense materials, typically wood or metal posts, they pull energy from the surrounding area and send it downward. You may experience an overall drain on the immune system, since the time your body normally spends relaxing and rebuilding is spent combatting the beam. Even if you have to move your bed or couch to a less than opportune place, keep it out from under the beam.

The energy from these ceiling beams interacts with the bed occupant throughout the night. Covering the beams or a canopy bed may alleviate the pressure of the energy.

The painted waves on this beam visually lift your energy.

If bamboo flutes do not match the decor of your home or your symbolic system, try these:

▲ Paint the beam the same color as the ceiling to wrap energy around the beam instead of sending it down.

▲ Trail a living plant such as ivy along the beam to soften chi flow.

▲ Paint something (vines, coat of arms, flowers, or angels) on the beam to visually lift energy. This will train your body to respond differently to the presence of the beam.

▲ Use angels positioned at 45-degree angles on the beam sides. Energy moves in a default pattern unless acted upon by your intent. Intent alone can soften and disperse energy from the beam. Angels are strong reminders of that intent.

▲ If the beam is in your bedroom, move energy upward with a four-poster bed.

▲ Drape netting, gauze, or a swag over your bed. This literally carries energy across the top and sends it cascading down the sides where it will not harm you.

▲ If the beam is in your living room, use a plant such as a palm tree and position it so that the leaves arch up and above the seating area.

What to do if you cannot avoid the beam. Since a beam causes a strong downward push, adjust for it by placing objects that either move the energy upwards or spread it out. The traditional Chinese adjustment for shifting the energy from a beam is to hang two bamboo flutes at 45-degree angles on the beam, lifting the downward-moving chi. Bamboo flutes have numerous cultural associations and can be powerful adjustments.

If your bed is under a beam, drape a cloth over the top, directing energy across the bed and down the side, away from the body.

Slanted, exposed & vaulted ceilings

Whenever you enter a room, you automatically extend your energy upward to find the ceiling. Once this relationship is established, you use it to stabilize your movements through the room. If the ceiling slants or if the beams are exposed, you constantly adjust your own auric field to remain "in relationship" with the ceiling.

Most homes do not have exposed ceilings, but many have slanted ones. While it is true that a slanted ceiling will elevate your chi, it can be quite disrupting, especially in bedrooms. You can do much with your furniture to balance the volatile energy flow that results from a slanted ceiling.

It is especially important to place something tall in the corners. Put pictures on this wall of anything that moves up, such as butterflies, balloons, planes, flying birds, or trees. If your pictures contain geometric shapes, make certain the shapes expand at the top. Live plants and lights on this side of the room will lift the energy and help the entire room feel more balanced.

On the wall with the highest ceiling, hang a tapestry or picture that directs energy down. You can tell which direction energy moves by following your eye movements. If your eye moves down when you look at a picture, then energy moves down. If your eye starts somewhere in the middle and then moves up when you look at it, the picture is directing energy up. Positioning heavier furniture pieces on this side of the room will hold energy more stable.

Place items with a strong upward movement, such as lamps, tall chests, or upward-moving plants, on the wall with the lowest ceiling.

The low, cushioned couches create much needed stability for a room with a vaulted ceiling.

Windows

Windows let in vital natural sunlight, but depending on the time of day and your needs, you might not want to sit in front of them. A general rule of feng shui is to protect your back and windows provide less protection than a solid wall. However, during the day when light comes in the window, sitting with your back to the window will supply vital chi through the chakras on the top of your head and the back of your neck. In the evening, the chi flow reverses and a seat by the window will start to drain your chi.

▲ Use inset panes to break up large windows and keep chi from flowing out.

▲ Be certain to use coverings in the evening to keep chi in.

▲ Be aware of what you see through your window. The view is as important as the window itself.

If you must place a chair next to a window, make certain the windows have thick curtains that can be closed in the evening to minimize the chi drain.

Ceiling fans

A ceiling fan drastically affects your chi. As each blade cuts through your aura, your body sends energy out to restore its structure and balance. In the bedroom, when six to ten blades per second are slicing through your aura, it takes a lot of energy to keep reconstructing your field. As a result, you wake up feeling drained, bruises take longer to go away, colds seem to linger, and cuts heal slowly.

If you need a fan to cool things off, use a floor fan and direct the blades away from your body. Use fans in adjacent rooms, rather than turning them on in the room that you are currently in. In the bedroom, you can turn on your ceiling fan before you go to bed to cool things off and then turn it off while you are sleeping under it. However, even when they are not on, the blades affect you.

A round faceted crystal can be added to your pullcord to disperse energy from a ceiling fan's blades and soften their constant effect on the body.

Because this ceiling fan is not directly above the desk, it actually helps stabilize energy in the room by diverting the strong chi flowing down with the slanted ceiling.

Chi experiment:

1. Stand under a flat ceiling and hold one arm down at your side, the other one straight out to your side.

2. Have someone push down on the extended arm while you resist. You should get a good idea of how strong you are by how much you are able to resist.

3. Now, turn the fan on and stand directly underneath it.

4. Have someone do exactly the same thing with your extended arm as before. (Your friend should not stand under the fan when doing this or his own strength will be diminished.) Notice how your physical strength decreases when under the fan.

Avoid placing breakable items, such as a glass table, under a chandelier to reduce its threatening impact.

Chandeliers

Any heavy object hanging over your head creates an oppressive and foreboding reaction in the body. Remember, in feng shui, the potential of danger can affect the psyche just as much as if something had actually occurred.

Exchanging a heavy light fixture for one that connotes buoyancy and lift like this one helps people feel safer seated around a glass table.

The uneven ceiling and sharp corner edges in this room create a volatile chi flow, making it difficult to feel balanced and safe. The competing attention of the large windows, the ceiling fan, and the pillars sends a feeling of confusion.

Sharp corners

When choosing between two possible placements, look around the room and see if there are any sharp angles (two walls coming together, the edge of a dresser or armoire, a plant stand, or floor-to-ceiling pillar) that point directly at you and where you will be sitting. This particular situation, referred to as "poison arrows," creates an intense flow of energy that is three to four times as strong as what comes off of a flat wall. This drains energy from the physical body because the body has to send energy out into your auric field to balance the pressure of the energy that is pointed at you. The more intense the angle, the more it disrupts your personal chi flow.

When you unconsciously position yourself at the end of a sharp point, it can reveal a tendency to place yourself at risk to smooth things out for others. It can also indicate counterintentions that undermine your goals.

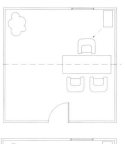

The placement of furniture in this home office drains chi from the person seated behind the desk because the filing cabinet angle creates a poison arrow.

Simply moving the desk to the other side of the room shifts the angle of the filing cabinet and eliminates the draining effect of the poison arrow.

Numerology & arrangement

Numbers represent organic energy patterns. It feels different to place one candle by itself in the middle of the table than it does to group three candles together. Even though both create fire energy, the amount of candles on the table changes the pattern. By consciously evoking the patterns of the numbers one through nine you can change the way you feel when you are in a room.

Odd vs. even

Regardless of the specific number, the general categories of odd and even have common characteristics. Even numbers generate a yin pattern. They contract energy, slow it down, and stabilize it. Odd numbers are more yang in nature. They expand energy, push against boundaries, and open up possibilities and conversations. If you find you are partial to two of this and four of that, you probably prefer things that are predictable, safe, and structured. If your preference is for groupings of three or five, chances are that stability is not as important as fun, creativity, and growth.

One of something increases the energy of self-sufficiency.

This room balances odd- and even-numbered placements to keep chi flowing in an auspicious way. The two matching lamps and candle sconces stabilize the single picture over the mantel. The third sofa keeps the seating interesting.

Singles

One of something encourages alone time. It creates a partial separation between that item and everything else in the universe. If your child has a tendency to isolate himself at school, a single chair or a single poster in his room will compound feelings of isolation. On the other hand, if it is difficult to enforce a healthy sense of boundaries, use single placements to energetically break codependent ties and encourage autonomy.

Take notice of how many solitary objects are sprinkled throughout your living space. When you get used to living life as a "party of one," you arrange your furniture differently. When someone does come over, you might need to scramble to find another chair or another toothbrush. When your physical space closes up, so does your body. To open your body again, start by opening up your space. Place two chairs side-by-side or two pillows on your bed. Hang up pictures with more than one person in them. Experience how it feels to take down a single picture and hang an entire grouping of pictures, even better if the pictures are of other significant people in your life: friends, siblings, mentors, parents, and children.

When there are only two of something, it is by nature more intimate. An arrangement of two draws people together.

The three items in the picture, as well as the three coins and three items on the dresser, represent heaven, man, and earth.

Twosomes

Partners come in twos. Arranging your home in groups of two draws your attention and your energy to your partnerships. When there are only two of something, it is by nature more intimate. An arrangement of two draws people together. Two chairs, a love seat just big enough for two, two table-side lamps, two wooden ducks on the mantel, two pictures above the couch all send a message to the brain to form partnerships. Grouping your furniture together in twosomes encourages harmony, diplomacy, and gentleness. Conversations tend to be quiet, soft, and flowing.

Note: *If you are just leaving a relationship and need to reestablish your own grounding (your identity as a unit of one), it can help to remove some of those twosomes for a while, especially if the items hold the energy of the previous partner.*

Dynamics of three

The three points of the triangle are key in understanding the energy of the number three. Three represents the union of heaven, man, and earth, as well as the union of body, mind, and spirit. It is an active number. It sets things on an angle, encourages a look at the unusual, and finds humor in the situation.

Groupings of three bring fire energy into your home. Seating for three heats up conversations. Three colors or three textures in a room add spark, interest, and fun. Three windows bring in more light, more social gaiety, and more sexual energy.

Because the energy of three is always moving out and always expanding, too many threes in your space can put you on edge and deplete your finances faster.

Four chairs feel stable and safe. The four corners of the rectangular table add to the stability.

Five brightly colored sachets are an easy way to bring adventure into any room.

Stability of four

The number four holds the energy pattern of the square. Squares are secure, safe, and stable. They form the foundation of every building. Rooms have four walls, beds have four posts, chairs have four legs. Combinations of four help us feel confident that we are okay and the world is a safe place. Groupings of four encourage good study and work habits, steady employment, and financial security. The number four is also closely related to the nurturing and supporting energy of mother earth.

By placing two couches across from each other, you are bringing the energy of the square into your living room. A four-drawer filing cabinet in your office will encourage you to be more organized and work hard. Four chairs at the kitchen table will help people feel more grounded when they sit there. Four plants in a room will remind you to slow down, take your time, and be practical. Increase groupings of four when life starts to feel crazy, or too fast.

Excitement of five

The number five generates creative and social energy. Pushing energy out in all directions, fives break through boundaries, defy conventions and containment, and make room for new adventures. If you like arrangements of five, you probably do not think of yourself as ordinary. Safety is nice, but not at the expense of excitement. A fifth side or wall will throw people off base and confuse them because they are expecting four. Living room groupings for five will stimulate conversation, but people will not stay seated for long.

Fives are usually digested best in small quantities. For a little excitement without turning your world upside down, try five tiki torches in the yard, five canisters on the kitchen counter, or five pillows on your bed. Hanging pictures of flowers with five petals is a subtle way to bring adventure into your home and a stack of five magazines or folded towels in the bathroom will feel stimulating and luxurious.

Six items gather people together as family. These soap rocks are great in any room. They function not only as actual soap, but as a symbol of grounding and communal support.

Candlesticks work well in a grouping of seven because they represent transformation. Be certain to light them at least once a week.

Nurturing support of six

Six is the vibration of family. In feng shui, an arrangement of six represents grandfather, grandmother, father, mother, oldest son, and oldest daughter. Arrangements of six foster respect for others opinions, for the earth from which we all come, and for the diversity of the human family. Six chairs around the dining table will help gather families together. A family picture gallery with six pictures brings harmony into familial relations.

A six vibration is also drawn to beautiful things, to the creation of art, and any expression of the heart. Try six different flower varieties in your next floral arrangement. Hang six coffee cups or plates on your display rack, or place six stones in your garden path.

Spirituality of seven

Seven is a mystical number symbolizing a connection to universal energies. The biblical reference to the creation of the world represents seven days. There are seven major chakras in the body. When you enter a seven vibration, you place yourself in a spiritual vortex, a place devoted to contemplation and awakening. Seven Buddhas in your meditation area or seven candles on your altar will forever change its energy. Praying for a dedicated purpose for seven days has an ethereal power. Seven rocks in a bowl or a Zen garden, seven flowers in a vase, or seven books in a reading nook will all encourage a stronger connection to intuition, deep meditation, and metaphysical studies.

An eight-sided ba gua mirror is an excellent way to promote harmony and balance. The shape is exactly half a circle and half a square, the perfect balance between yin and yang. The octagon represents abundance in Chinese cultures because the word for eight sounds like the word for prosperity.

Groupings of nine will enhance the energy of any meditation room because they generate the energy pattern of transcendence. Nine represents completion and the ushering forth of a new cycle.

Abundance of eight

For the Chinese, money comes in bundles of eight. Eight black goldfish, eight coins, and eight items on a mobile are all traditional arrangements for calling forth material abundance. You can place eight stones in your fountain, eight wind chimes on your porch, or eight fish in your aquarium to evoke the energy pattern of abundance in your home. An arrangement of eight connotes authority, a good business sense, financial success, and balance between yin and yang. Arrangements of eight will encourage you to work hard and exert discipline in your endeavors. If you are feeling lazy or adrift, a ritual of lighting eight candles once a day for eight days can call forth your will power.

Completion of nine

Nine is the most auspicious of all numbers in feng shui because it represents the completion of one cycle and the initiation of a new cycle. Nine is the big picture number, and as such, calls forth compassion and wisdom. You can augment your feng shui adjustments by incorporating the number nine when performing the adjustment. For example, when you hang a crystal by a ribbon, cut the ribbon to a length of 18 or 27 inches. When burning candles to activate an area of the ba gua, burn nine candles. The actions signal your intent to welcome new energy patterns into your life.

Tracking chi flow through a room

Once you track the chi flow, avoiding certain placements becomes obvious. Placing furniture in the mouth of chi creates an uncomfortable situation.

1. **Locate primary door.** The main door is the mouth of chi and the primary source of energy. Chi will flow directly towards walls and windows. If there is a door or a window opposite the main door, most of your chi will flow directly through the room and out.

2. **Look for blocking furniture.** Check to see if your furniture blocks the flow of chi through the room.

3. **Rearrange furniture to be compatible with chi flow.** Use your furniture to draw chi further into the room, instead of blocking it. Move your furniture to the side of the main chi path.

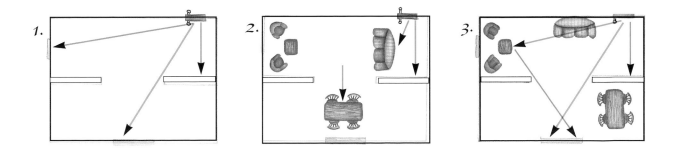

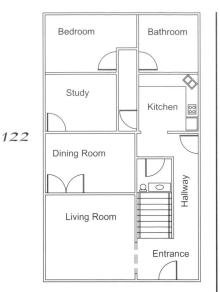

This closed floor plan blocks the flow of energy, and discourages unity and cooperation among the inhabitants.

Closed floor plan

A Victorian house epitomizes a closed floor plan. Victorians valued privacy and boundaries, therefore each passageway had an actual door. Because of all the doors, furniture placement became difficult. When rooms are completely separate, the inhabitants are left feeling separate from each other. They lose the flow of a harmonious whole.

Reclaiming floor space. Visually or physically remove doors without energetically blocking passageways. If at all possible, exchange doors that open in or out for doors that slide sideways.

One-way traffic. When traffic flows in two directions through a crowded space, energy gets jumbled and causes confusion. Determine an optimal path for the energy flow through your house. Then use furniture and picture placement to direct people to move in the desired path.

The wall down the middle. Many floor plans have a wall or hallway down the middle of the house. This divides the energy of the house into two separate patterns and influences communication patterns between family members. When you physically live in separate worlds, you are not inclined to communicate as openly and as intimately as you would otherwise.

In a room with lots of doors, consider placing a folding screen in front of an unused door to create a temporary wall. This will give you more options for placing furniture in the room.

To unite a room, choose a warm neutral color to spread light (and energy) equally throughout.

Energetically uniting the house

Color. When you have a closed floor plan, it is especially important to visually integrate your home. The easiest and most influential way to do this is to paint the entire interior of the house the same color or at least stay with the same color palette. Interestingly, Victorians traditionally used paint to even further separate the rooms of the house, the parlor was red while the dining room was green and the bedroom blue. Cool colors will cause spaces to draw apart from each other while warm colors will draw them closer together.

Decor. A common decor style and furniture period will energetically unite the house. Although it is possible, it is difficult to pull furniture from different periods together and increase chi flow at the same time. Each period has an energetic pattern that is generated by the shape, size, and style of the piece.

Lighting. Another way to encourage an even flow of chi through the space is to have the same amount of lighting in each room. When one room is considerably darker or lighter than another, they separate energetically.

An unused doorway, which was to the left of this couch, is now covered by useful shelves, which transformed this area from a walkway into a comfortable sitting room.

Open floor plan

Contemporary design typically considers the open floor plan to be ideal. The light and open spaces create a less restrictive closed-off floor plan. However, open floor plans have their own issues that need to be considered and adjusted.

Open is great, but this open floor plan brings an overwhelming flow of chi directly into the room. There is no opportunity to make the transition from the outside to a comfortable settling.

The room becomes more inviting by placing a screen between the entryway and the living room to create a transition area. The plant at the end of the screen softens the edge and moves chi upward. The added half-walls between the kitchen and the TV room, as well as between the living room and the breakfast nook, bring stability and peace into the rooms.

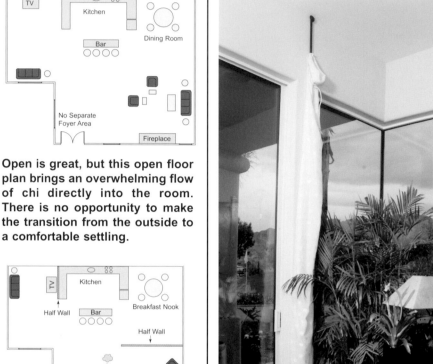

The addition of a screen allows for better placement of furniture and provides more privacy for the inhabitants.

To add stability in a room:
- ▲ Use large furniture pieces with padded arms.
- ▲ Hang pictures in a horizontal line.
- ▲ Use darker colors on floor than walls or ceiling.
- ▲ Use same carpeting on all levels of your house.
- ▲ Fill in open banisters or railings.
- ▲ Make certain all stairs have closed runners.
- ▲ Use large heavy objects at bottom of staircases.
- ▲ Place calming pictures at bottom of staircases.

The carpeted stairs and thick rug at the bottom of the stairs stabilize the fast volatile chi of this open staircase.

The amoebae effect. Open floor plans make it difficult to create spaces that feel separate from the rest of the house. In this situation, you often feel as though no matter where you go, you cannot get away from everyone and everything else going on in the house. Consider replacing an open doorway with a door that can shut. You can also hang a drape to visually close off the space or use plants or folding screens to section off different areas. Choosing different colors and decor styles for different sections of the house will create a partial separation, but still leave things open and flowing.

Too much too fast. With open floor plans, energy speeds up considerably. If life starts feeling crazy and things are happening too quickly, slow things down by using large heavy pieces of furniture. Use textured walls, textured fabrics, and dark or muted colors. Carpet floors or use large thick rugs (preferably rugs with simple patterns). Provide the ability to dim the lights and use window coverings that can block out the sunlight and chi if necessary.

Too many levels. Another characteristic of an open floor plan is a multileveled house in which you are constantly moving up or down as you move through the house. This constant movement makes it very difficult for people to feel grounded in the house, especially children. This lack of grounding manifests in two primary ways. Either people will have a difficult time settling down, attending to details, and staying focused on a task; or they will try to ground themselves with piles of clutter, especially paper. If you find yourself pulled from one thing to another from the minute you wake up in the morning, chances are your house does not help you feel grounded. But, you can create grounding without opting for clutter.

Interior doors that do not line up cause a distorted view of an interior room and cause an uneasiness in occupants.

Directing the flow of chi

If you could watch a sped-up movie of your family's movements throughout the day, you would have a good sense of how chi flows through your home. Interior doors, furniture, and floor coverings are key elements that guide us through each space, speed us up, and slow us down.

Interior doors

Offset doors. Interior doors that do not line up are fine unless they are across a narrow hall from each other. Such doors create a distorted view. When entering or leaving one room, you see partially into the other, but not fully and completely. When your view is distorted, so is brain function. The traditional adjustment for this situation is to place a mirror or picture on the side of the door so that the mirror or picture lines up with the edge of the door opposite it. This will give the one eye more to look at than a blank wall and stabilizes depth perception accordingly.

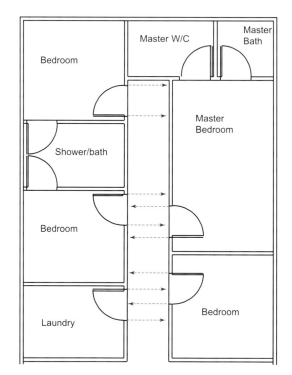

When doors in a narrow hallway do not line up evenly, you get a distorted view into one room when coming out of another. One eye sends your brain one message and the other eye sends a different message. This creates instability and confusion in the body.

To correct the straight shot, stagger items on alternating sides of the room or hallway to simulate a curving path. If you do not have room along the sides, use eye-catching pictures to draw chi sideways as people walk through the area. The low shelf in this photograph also helps keep chi from flowing out the windows.

The straight shot. When doorways line up with each other, it is a straight shot. The straight shot allows chi to travel quickly and straight through a room. Sitting in the path of chi is not comfortable. The best adjustment for this situation is to place items such as a plant or a folding screen on the sides of the chi path to coax the straight column of energy into a wave pattern.

This chair placement blocks chi from flowing through the doorway. This translates into blocked opportunities for the inhabitants.

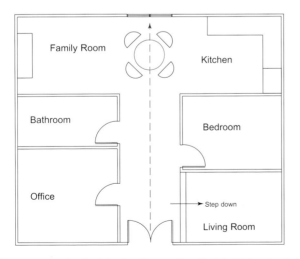

Be aware of what is in the path of chi. This straight shot from the front door travels right into the dining room table. This creates an uncomfortable feeling for those seated around the table.

Blocked doors. Doors that are physically blocked by stacks of boxes or furniture have a blocking effect in your psyche.

Furniture placement

Facing your guests. More energy flows out from the front of the furniture than from the back. Therefore, when you turn a piece of furniture toward someone, you engage the chi of the person. This energetic relationship plays out in different ways. For example, it takes less energy to walk into the embrace of a seating arrangement than it does to walk around the back, even though it might take the same amount of steps.

This arrangement is open to the front door, but has its back to the kitchen. Although this may seem ideal when entertaining, guests assemble in the kitchen even if they are crammed, because they feel segregated in the living room.

When the furniture arrangement was changed so the chi flowed naturally from the kitchen, through the dining room, and into the living room, guests flowed from room to room, allowing chi to flow as well.

Floor coverings. Certain floor coverings are more yang and speed up chi flow, others are more yin and slow things down. When you incorporate yin flooring choices, such as rugs and carpets, you encourage people to sit down and relax. Hardwood floors and tile work well for walkways and areas where you want people to keep moving. An entire room of hardwood or tile flooring with no rugs leaves people looking for a place to rest. Use rugs under your conversation areas to provide grounding and to slow the chi for people to feel comfortable. In addition to anchoring conversation areas, rugs are key elements in directing traffic flow.

Although you do not consciously look down, you automatically move in whatever direction the rug is angled. In these photographs, the first rug placement leads people right into the mirror wall, the second placement guides them into the next room. If you want people to enter one room rather than another when they come into your house, angle the rug in the entryway to direct them. If you have one view that is better than another, angling the rug will automatically turn people toward the better view.

Furniture density. Furniture density is the proportion of furniture in a room to clear open space. Measure your walkways. If the pass-through areas between pieces of furniture are less than 36 inches wide, you have too much furniture in too small of a space. If your furniture is too close together, people will contract more energy than they expand and not relax. Over time, your family and friends will be more stressed, more uptight, and more on edge than they would be otherwise. As a general rule, the furniture in a room should only take up ⅓ to ½ of the space.

The room above is overcrowded, making it harder for chi to flow. In the photograph below, the removal of a few items has made a considerable difference in the density factor of this room. The abundant quality still exists, yet the room is not overpowered by too many things.

Window corners have the opposite problem from wall corners. Instead of chi stagnating, it is funneled into the corner and out the window. Remedy this by planting trees and shrubs outside the window to slow the chi down as it leaves the house.

Corners. The two walls on either side of a corner push energy in and create a pressurized area where it is difficult for energy to move freely. It tends to get blocked and stuck. Some people instinctively place their furniture on an angle, trying to take care of this problem. If nothing is between the corner and the angled furniture, however, the blocked chi builds and pushes out on the seating area. People feel pushed out of their seats just as they would if there were too many pillows behind their back.

There is nothing wrong with angling furniture. A 45-degree angle imitates part of a ba gua shape, which promotes a balanced flow that is not too fast or too slow. However, this only works if you deal with your corners. Place a large standing plant or a lamp between the corner and the sofa.

To alleviate the pressure of a corner, place a corner piece such as this dish cupboard.

Area solutions

The front door

Your front entrance greets society every day. More than any other entrance feature, the door conveys messages about who you are, what's important to you, and how you would like others to interact with you. As with every aspect of feng shui, the objective is to match the vibration of the entryway with the people living in the home. The more awareness you bring to choices such as "What color should I paint the front door?", the more you can transform your home into a reflection of your best and highest self.

The size, quality, and overall condition of your door reflects your social position and status. Money has a distinct energy pattern. That is why money attracts money and prestige attracts prestige. To shift the way the world interacts with you, you need to change the energy pattern of the entrance.

To welcome abundance, be certain your front door is in good repair. Keep the door and frame clean and metal polished.

To activate energy in the entryway with natural light, add flat leaded panes or stained-glass windows.

Draw the chi of money

If you have a single-width door, visually extend the door by placing chi activators on both sides of it. Use brightly colored flowers around the front door to extend the chi sideways.

Doorbells and door knockers connote the personality and social stature of the owner. The house number holds an energetic pattern that affects the entire house. To draw more prominence to the house, get larger numbers and use a material that reflects light, such as brass, bronze, or copper.

Even if you do not use your front door as your normal entrance, it is still the energetic face of your house, therefore the mouth of chi. To balance out energy flowing into your home from different doors, make certain the front door gets opened at least once a day and that fresh air and sunlight are allowed to pass through the door.

To balance energy in a room, place an activator such as this radiometer, a light catcher, a mobile, or plants.

Link the energy of abundance to your entrance by placing an object that represents abundance to you, such as these coins, in both the entryway and the actual Abundance sector of the house.

If the door indents and is hard to see, you can pull chi forward by placing the chi activators further out on the porch.

Choosing a front door color

You do not have to paint your door Chinese red for it to be good feng shui; but whatever color you choose will have an impact on the chi of the entire house. Because your front door represents the face you present to the external world, the color of the door will attract certain energies and avert others. Painting the front door is an inexpensive way to attract energy to your home to support your current life purpose. Consider changing the color of your front door at least once a year and make certain that it is sending the correct message to the world. Last year's color might not work to fulfill this year's dreams.

New growth colors inspire and stimulate change.

Stabilizing colors increase feelings of safety.

Relaxing colors mark a home as a peaceful retreat.

Activator colors get chi moving and bring something new into your life.

If you want the house to be welcoming, be certain house numbers are lit and visible from the street.

Lot size & features. If you have a large lot and your house tends to get lost on it, the door needs a lot of punch. Brown, black, or white is not going to work well for you. A house that sits prominently on the lot can benefit from more subtle colors.

If the lot slopes, avoid colors that create a water vibration such as black, cool blues, and blue-greens. A stabilizing earth influence such as browns, yellows, and terra-cotta are helpful for sloped lots. If the slope is extreme, choose a color with an intense wood or fire vibration that will shoot energy upward.

Because this house already dominates the lot, the subdued brown color helps restore balance.

Placing a windchime between the street and your front door will provide protection and safety.

To initiate a change in career, choose a door color that has the same energy as the career you want to move into:
▲ Counseling
▲ Sales
▲ Marketing
▲ Healing
▲ Service-oriented
▲ Entertainment
▲ Computers
▲ Design

Career needs. If your front door is in your Journey sector, make certain that the color you choose for the door is in harmony with your chosen career. If you have a high-profile career, you do not want a subtle front door. Drama and contrast will create the energetic push you need. Use more than one color on your door or add more lighting to make things zing. To calm stress in your chosen career, opt for muted colors in a more natural palette.

House color & materials. Your door should balance the energy of the rest of the house. If the house is bright and dramatic, the door should provide relief. If the house is neutral and subdued, the door should provide some excitement and the hint of the unexpected. Brick houses are already grounded and earthy and would benefit from a bright fire door. Wood houses support growth and upward movement and can be balanced by a water vibration.

If your house sits close to the street, create more privacy by choosing a subtle door color or by setting the door in a recessed alcove.

House guardians

Wind chimes have been used for centuries to protect homes and temples from spirits. Through sound, wind chimes warn of a shift in energy. Coconut and bamboo chimes work well as guardians because the hollow spaces represent psychic protection against the unknown. Metal chimes have the clearest sound and balance energy in the body.

Dragons placed outside your home are an excellent protection symbol. Some dragons have a specific calling and blessing that they bestow on the house.

Frogs placed outside your home symbolize the arrival of prosperity and abundance.

Tortoises represent the steady development of a satisfying career that is built on compassion and consideration for your well-being and the well-being of others.

House guardian symbols of safety and protection can change as your needs change. Any winged guardian can protect you from assaults that affect your place in the community.

Whatever you choose to place in your entrance space sets the energy for the entire home.

The turtle as a house guardian symbolizes the steady increase of career chi and financial stability.

This glass door allows natural light into the home. The area rugs direct traffic into the main area of the house and away from a private office doorway. The two chairs to the side promote hospitality. The treasures in the curio cabinet personalize an otherwise austere setting.

Entry lighting

Lighting should be considered carefully. Natural light eases the transition, making it easier for your eyes and your energy to adjust to interior light. If it is not possible to allow natural light into the space, use full-spectrum lighting in the entry. It will also help if your entry is one of the lightest spaces in the house. You feel more comfortable when the shift from bright outdoor light to dim interior light is gradual rather than abrupt.

Inside the door

The entrance provides a place to transition from the outside world (a yang state) to your personal space (a yin state). If you walk through your front door straight into your living room, the transition feels abrupt and harsh. Consider building a half wall or create a divider with a folding screen, a wall of plants, or even a sofa table. This area should hold items that allow the transition from outside to inside to flow smoothly.

Track lighting is an easy way to increase overall illumination in an entry.

Placing shiny objects behind your burners allows you to keep involved with the rest of the room when your back is turned.

Display an abundance of spices and oils and use them regularly. If you need to have your knives on the counter, be certain they are safely ensconced in a wood block, rather than hanging them from a magnetic strip.

The stove

The stove allows you to nurture yourself and provide for your physical needs. In many cultural traditions, the stove houses gods that watch out for your overall health and physical strength. Before stoves, the hearth or campfire represented the state of the family's physical well-being. As long as the fire was burning strong, the family's personal chi would also be strong.

When preparing food, you want to feel as comfortable and secure as possible. Whatever energy state you are in when you are cooking is passed directly into the food. Nothing absorbs negative emotions or stress more than food and water. If you are feeling out of sorts, grumpy, or stressed while preparing dinner, take a few seconds and run your hands under warm water. Running water can pull negativity and stress out of your body and release it down the drain. You will feel more relaxed and balanced, and the entire cooking/dining experience will improve.

The openings over the sink help those in the kitchen feel more involved with guests in the adjoining living room.

Stove placement & use

If you stand with your back to the room while preparing meals, it is hard to be visually and energetically a part of what is going on in the rest of the kitchen. If possible, position your stove so you are facing the room. This may require an island or an L-shaped counter. If you cannot face the room, try to provide a side view of the comings and goings. A traditional adjustment is to place a convex mirror on the wall behind the stove. This works great if you do not have a range top or hood above the stove. Another great fix is a shiny curved teapot.

Use all four burners. The stove is the central fire element in your house. If you only use the front burners, or none at all, you send yourself the message that you only want access to part of your energy reserves. Leaving a teapot full of water on the stove is another way to weaken this fire element, since water subdues the energy of fire. Move your teapot around to all four burners and empty the water out when you are done.

Keep it clean. Because your stove represents your physical health and well-being, keeping it clean reflects directly on your desire to care for your physical body. A clean stove keeps chi flowing smoothly and does not allow for stagnation.

An island in the kitchen, containing the stove, gives the cook the opportunity to be involved with guests in the rest of the room while cooking.

The rounded counter in this kitchen keeps chi flowing around the counter and connotes the auspicious ba gua shape.

Countertops

No matter what your countertops are made of, watch your edges. A flat edge can create a sharp arrow pointing right at you when you stand at the stove or sink. Use dowsing rods to measure the extent to which any sharp edges in your kitchen cut your chi. This is crucial if your countertops are made of granite or some other sharp material. Your desire to be in and cook in your kitchen will diminish greatly. To strengthen your chi and create an environment of support and physical nurturing, invest in double-rounded edges for all countertops. Although the single round is better than a flat edge, it still carries an undercurrent of sharpness.

Placing plants and upward items in the corner behind the sink will slow down chi leaving through the window.

The microwave placed next to this refrigerator creates conflicting chi.

Balancing fire & water

Sometimes the stove is next to the refrigerator or sink. These both carry a strong downward water vibration and are in conflict with the upward expansive energy of fire. To balance water and fire, place something wood between the stove and the water element. Wooden cabinets, cutting boards, even cooking utensils can all help create a balanced flow of energy instead of an abrupt transition. Also, be certain the microwave does not sit next to a water element.

The granite countertop balances the volatile chi of the sink placed next to the stovetop.

Things hanging overhead

Pots and pans. Think about the desirability of this situation. A bunch of large heavy unstable pots hanging over your head is not going to create an environment of safety, stability, and comfort. Just stand under your pot rack, turn your head up and look at all those pots. Do you really want the sensation of things hanging over your head?

If you need to keep the pot rack above your head, do not leave any of the hooks empty. Empty hooks represent a tendency to allow the moods and actions of others to trigger undesired responses. You are symbolically leaving yourself open to being caught by psychic traps, jabs, and pulls. Make certain that the hooks themselves are rounded, rather than sharp points.

This kitchen demonstrates a precarious situation with pans hanging directly over the cooks head.

This kitchen provides a practical way to store and display pots and kitchen items without hanging them.

The matching lamps and nightstands represent equality in the relationship. The pillars to the side of the bed draw the blessings of heaven into this union.

Even a nightlight can be symbolic. This one represents long life.

The bed

Clear energies from previous relationships

Objects from previous relationships hold energy from that relationship and can greatly undermine your efforts to do things differently in a new relationship. If at all possible, start a new relationship in a home that is new to both of you. There is nothing more unsettling than moving into someone's house. They might be saying "I love you, please move in," but their space says "Sorry, I'm already full of someone else's energy, habits, emotions, and tendencies."

If starting out somewhere new to both of you is impossible, making a few changes to the old home will bring harmony to the new relationship. It is crucial to start a new intimate relationship with a new mattress set. You are more vulnerable and intimate in bed than any other location, and the mattress holds the vibrations from whatever has transpired in that bed (especially a waterbed).

The bed frame, especially the headboard, represents how you and your partner support each other. If you want to do things differently in the new relationship, get a new headboard.

Surround yourself with sensuality

The most arousing thing to a man is a passionate woman. Therefore, women, do not feel selfish placing things that please you in your bedroom. If it puts you in touch with your sensual nature, he will appreciate it. Small additions like plush towels, new sheets, or erotic scents can have a big impact on how sensual you feel.

Choosing the right bed

Beds carry different vibrations. Shape, color, and materials influence ambiance. Choose a bed with the right energetic impact for you.

Bed shapes. Fire vibrations are not generally recommended for beds. Stay away from triangular-shaped headboards. Triangular shapes in your bedroom encourage triads in your relationship. The triad can manifest in the form of an affair. This also means do not place your bed on a diagonal, since that creates a triangle directly behind your head.

Flowers, oils, and candles have a long psychological association with romance that may or may not light your fire.

The combination of this water element sleigh bed and the red fire comforter bring a balance of warmth and strength.

Earth vibration. A bed with an earth vibration will help you ground. It increases feelings of safety and support. Any bed with a solid wooden headboard creates an earth vibration, remember the headboard represents your psychological support system.

Bed textures & fabrics. Adding texture increases your awareness of your tactile sense, which puts you more in touch with your physical body. Soft textures in the bedroom encourage intimacy and the tendency to be kind to yourself and others. Cotton brings the natural world indoors and has a crisp clean energy. Silks and satins have a lush smoothness that allow energy to flow quickly. Chenille is nurturing and supportive. Use this to soften and comfort, but do not turn your bedroom into a therapist's couch.

Fabrics recommended for the bedroom:
▲ Cotton
▲ Silk
▲ Satin
▲ Chenille

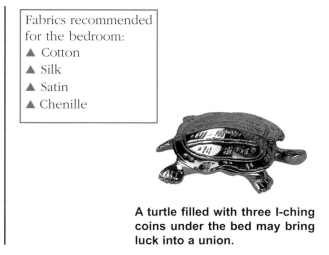

A turtle filled with three I-ching coins under the bed may bring luck into a union.

Bed colors. Warm tones encourage physical intimacy. Although cool colors are helpful for inducing sleep, if your walls cast a gray or blue on your skin you will not be inclined to intimacy. It is best to use soft tones, such as a light rose or terra-cotta, that cast warm hues on your skin without being too physically stimulating.

Use peach carefully. Peach is a volatile color that initiates change in the body. Only use peach if your relationship is in need of a shift. Add peach pillows or something you can remove when you want things to stabilize.

Use black sparingly. Black represents boundaries and separation, and black-and-white color schemes create literal lines of separation. If you feel the need for strong boundaries in order to feel safe in your relationship, use black and white. If boundaries are not something you want to emphasize, avoid this combination.

Display photographs of family in your bedroom in silver frames to encourage dreams of others.

Wood vibration. Beds with tall posts send energy upward and create a strong wood vibration.

A sunrise alarm clock stimulates a natural sunrise by slowly getting brighter and brighter within a 30 minute time frame. This allows you to wake up naturally, rather than being jolted awake.

Eastern light

If you are building a house and have a say as to where the bedrooms are positioned, consider facing your house to the south so the bedrooms are in the northeast-east corner. The body is better rested when it wakes up naturally. You can achieve this by placing your bed so that you can see the sunrise without the light falling directly on the bed. Waking up under the full light of the sun can get hot and uncomfortable at certain times of the year.

Water vibration. Beds with a water vibration such as a sleigh bed promote relaxation and release. Any bed with flowing or curving lines will help you let go of what you picked up today that you do not want to carry into tomorrow. Wicker headboards allow air to flow through and promote a water vibration. (Actual waterbeds are not advised however, since the water in them is usually chemically treated and is rarely replaced often enough to prevent stagnant chi.

Bedroom lighting

Choose lighting that complements your skin tone and shows off your body. Not many people have a body that can withstand the scrutiny of harsh daylight, so remember this when you are thinking about how many windows you want and what type of window treatments you are going to have displayed.

Use diffused, soft lighting in the bedroom to complement your skin appearance, as well as assist in relaxing your body.

Metal vibration. Metal beds pull energy into the center and are best suited for someone needing to gather their energy at the end of a stressful day. Sales people, therapists, or anyone who sends energy out in many directions during the day can benefit from the focusing effect of a metal bed. Many metal beds do not have a solid headboard, however. Weigh the benefits of the metal with the lack of solid support behind your head.

For the most relaxing situation, this bed is as far from the door as possible and behind the midline of the room. The closet doors on the left and the bathroom door on the right remain shut when not in use. The only solid wall is behind the head of the bed.

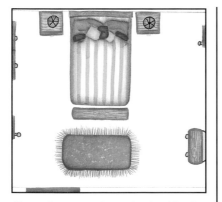

If you have to place the bed in the mouth of chi, use a rug or a hope chest at the foot of the bed to buffer chi. Keep the bathroom, closet and main door closed.

Place your bed with care

Place your bed in the room before anything else. Since most bedrooms are limited in possible placements, use the following prioritized list to avoid stressful situations.

Proximity to the door. Place the bed as far away from the door as possible and behind the midline of the room. If the door opens right onto the bed, chi from the rest of the house tends to rush in too quickly, making it difficult to settle down and fall asleep.

Adjustments: If it is not possible to get the bed away from the door, have a solid footboard and close the bedroom door an hour before bedtime to slow the flow of chi. You can also lessen the energy by placing a rug or chest in between the bed and the door.

If you have a window behind your bed, create the illusion of a wall with drapes.

A solid wall behind your head. Since energy travels more quickly through a window than through a solid wall, windows behind your head facilitate the transfer of your energy to the outside world. If you tend to get colds often or fatigue easily, support your immune system with a solid wall behind your head.

Adjustment: If you have to have a window at your head, be certain to use a solid headboard and place a pillow upright between your head and the headboard.

The metaphor of the nest works well in a bedroom where the couple nests in the shelter of each other.

Whether the bed is placed on a diagonal or against the wall, be careful not to stack things directly over the headboard.

Placing the bed at a diagonal. Avoid placing your bed on a diagonal. This creates a chasm directly behind your head, which greatly reduces how safe and supported you will feel in the bed. It also creates a more active chi flow in the room.

   Adjustment: If a diagonal placement is necessary because of ceiling beams or the shape of the room, be certain to fill the empty space with plants or a folding screen. Visually filling in the space will increase the sense that you are supported.

Because the only place for this bed was a diagonal placement, the upshooting plant behind the headboard keeps the chi from stagnating behind the bed.

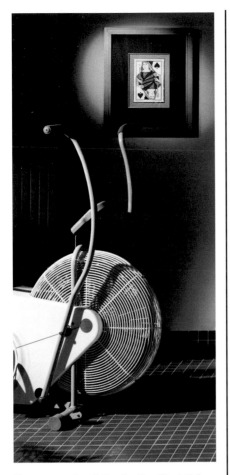

Overcrowding the bedroom

A common design error is over-crowding the bedroom. Sometimes this overcrowding comes with the addition of an exercise bike or desk, but sometimes it is the result of buying oversized imposing bedroom furniture. Your furniture should fit the space you are currently living in. Do not fall into the trap of thinking "We'll buy this big furniture now because some day we'll have a real master suite." This creates a dissonance between your current reality and a hoped-for reality. Create balance, harmony, and flow in your life today, and future realities become a mute point.

Your bed should not be more than ⅓ the size of the room and all your furnishings together should not take up more than half of the total space. Energy needs to flow easily through a bedroom for you to relax. This also means not storing items under the bed.

If an exercise bike is the first thing you see when you wake up, it is either a reminder of what you are not doing or an invitation to fulfill your needs for intimacy through a workout.

Coordinating items around the bed

The first thing you see in the morning will affect the energy you carry with you throughout the day. If you wake up looking at the toilet seat in the bathroom, imagine the effect that has on your day. If you first see when your desk, chances are you will have a harder time separating from work. If it is laundry pile you see, you will tend to focus on mundane tasks.

Overdoing it in a bedroom makes it difficult to rest and relax. Keep things simple here.

Use a battery-operated clock to reduce the EMF impact of an electric clock/radio.

Electronics by the bed. Electronics emit strong electromagnetic fields (EMFs) that artificially stimulate the body. The body has a natural EMF that aligns with the sun's. Man-made EMFs are much stronger and oscillate, moving back and forth through the body at up to 50 herz per second. It is difficult, if not impossible, to completely avoid EMFs throughout the day. Computers, refrigerators, and vacuum cleaners emit strong EMFs and are a part of every day reality. However, with some simple adjustments you can create an EMF-free zone in the bedroom. Spending those hours during which your body is most vulnerable and most receptive to its environment in an EMF-free zone can have astonishing benefits, including a more passionate sex life.

Covering as well as unplugging a television set when not in use will reduce EMF stimulation while the body is trying to relax.

A covered bedroom mirror will reduce the energy bouncing through the room, allowing a more peaceful sleep.

Mirrors in the bedroom

Mirrors in the bedroom keep energy active and make it more difficult to settle down and rest in the space. If you think this energy bouncing back and forth all night does not effect you, try an experiment. Cover the mirror with a thick drape each night for a week and leave them draped while you sleep. Use this week to see if you sleep more soundly and deeply when the mirror is covered. If you find this helps, use one of the following adjustments to buffer your body from the mirror at night.

If your partner wants to keep passion alive by keeping mirrors in the bedroom, use one of the following ideas to permanently buffer your body from active mirror chi at night.

▲ If the mirror is large and attached to the wall, use a folding screen positioned across the mirror in the evening. This way you can have full access to the mirror when you want it, but not worry about it otherwise.

▲ Consider a fabric panel or a pull drape that hangs from a tension rod. The fabric panel can be pulled to the side much like a window treatment during the day, but can cover the mirror at night. A pull drape can be attached to most any surface and can turn your mirror into a hidden delight.

▲ If your mirrors are on the front of closets opposite the bed, an easy and beautiful treatment is to have a glass company apply a white tint to your mirror. The white tint will actually turn the mirror opaque and you will not have as much energy bouncing around.

▲ If the mirror is on a stand, simply turn the mirror to face the wall while you are sleeping or drape a piece of fabric over it.

Energy attaches to moving water. If the toilet lid is left up, energy continually drains out of the house.

Taking worry out of bathrooms

Bathrooms have received a lot of bad press in feng shui books, most of which does not apply to the modern bathroom at all. In ancient times, there was no plumbing and bathrooms were such a smelly place that they were constructed as separate buildings from the house (a Chinese version of the outhouse). You definitely would not feel like eating a meal, cooking, or sleeping next to the kind of stench that was associated with the bathroom. Modern bathrooms do not have these same problems, but there are still some energy dynamics that you will want to be aware of.

The purpose of a bathroom is rejuvenation and release. We renew ourselves and get ready to meet each new day in the bathroom. We also let go of everything that our bodies no longer need there. Bathroom design should enhance these two functions.

After an intense argument or exchange of energy with another person, when you feel agitation or turmoil in your body, just standing under the shower head and letting hot water run down over your body is healing and restorative. Water acts as a magnet to draw toxic emotions out of your body, leaving you feeling renewed.

Many feng shui observations view the downward force of running water as a negative thing. Energy attaches itself to whatever has the most density, and water is more dense than air. Therefore, energy will attach itself to water and fall into a pattern of following the water down the pipes and away from your house. If too much energy leaves your house, it can cause a drain on the overall health and financial resources of the house.

The problem is, once the pattern is established, it continues until something breaks the pattern. Therefore, energy will continue to flow down and away even if the water is no longer running, until you break the pattern. Just putting down your toilet lid or closing the drain in your tub is enough to shift the flow of energy. You are directing it to stay rather than leave. Although too much downward flow is not healthy, the downward pull of running water helps the physical body release more than just dirt particles. It can pull positive ions off the body, which is a tremendous help in letting go of stress. It can also enhance the body's ability to release and let go of the energetic charge that accompanies certain emotions.

Baths can rejuvenate when you use bath salts or orange rinds to draw toxins out of your body. Orange rinds are known for their ability to help you release sorrow.

Intuition

Now that you have read an entire book to understand the principles that work in feng shui, it is important to stress the role of intuition in creating your living space. Intuition is a powerful sense of knowing whether something is right or not by connecting to a shared consciousness, an energetic force that transcends time and individual personalities. Many feng shui masters intentionally give their students conflicting advice to help them understand the power of intuition in reading the energy of a space.

What does intuition have to do with feng shui? Feng shui is a series of guidelines that work to put you in touch with your intuition, not replace it. Intuition is your permission to play. Try things out, see how they feel, and follow your intuition rather than rules. If the fountain feels better in the Family Heritage area of your home than it does in the Abundance area, trust that. Perhaps that familial

relationship needs more nurturing than your pocketbook at that time of your life. When I consult with clients and explain to them the positive impact of good choices they have made in placing their furnishings, they often comment "it just felt good there."

As you make your feng shui adjustments, be certain to pay attention to how your body feels. If you feel queezy in your stomach, you should replace the placement. If you hang a picture, for example, and you realize that you are feeling more distant, cut off from the rest of the world, rethink that adjustment. On the other hand, if you move your grandmother's piano to a certain corner of the living room and the music sounds brighter and crisper than it did before, you know you have made a change for the better. Let your body be your best guide. And if it tells you to put a hammock in your living room, trust it.

Acknowledgments

My mom and dad, for nurturing my spiritual and creative roots.

My sister Marla, for her professional organizing expertise and her unfaltering support.

My sister Marion, for her willingness to share candidly which aspects of feng shui were confusing to her.

My sister Leah Rae, for early lessons in color theory around the dining room table with a box full of crayons.

My dear friend Christine, for kindling the idea of writing a book, the Artist's Way support group, and for photographs of her beautiful home.

My dear friend Craig, for shouldering additional responsibilities cheerfully and for his encouragement and charm.

My sons Ryan and Austin, for bringing balance and joy into my daily life, reminding me to pause and breathe deeply.

My beloved Kent, for joining with me in spiritual partnership.

My dear friend Eileen, for providing a delightful sense of humor and emotional support.

Hydee and Kathryn, for the many hours they spent teaching me how to communicate through writing.

My editor Laura, who kept everything moving even when the rest of us needed a break.

My co-publisher Jo, who infused this project from start to finish with creativity and style.

The many clients and friends who graciously allowed us to photograph their homes, including Lisa Eyre, Janette Thomas, Kathy Lung, Fauntelle Young, Stephanie Nelson-Keith, Lisa Lundquist, Jo Packham, Christine Young, and Ryne Hazen.

Pat Nelson, for her amazing talents painting murals.

My brother Randon, for his photography saavy.

My many feng shui teachers for their consciousness-altering presence and feng shui wisdom.

Special thanks to the following artists and companies for sharing their exceptional products with our readers:

Pg 50 desk: Novikoff, Inc., Fort Worth, TX 800-780-0982
www.novikoff.com

Pg 63 bunkbed: Stanley Furniture, Stanleytown, VA 540-627-2000
www.stanleyfurniture.com

Pg 92 oval boxes: Charles Harvey

Pg 103 wooden chairs: Robert Sonday

Pg 108 desk: Century Furniture, Hickory, NC 828-326-8317
www.centuryfurniture.com

Pg 131 corner cupboard: Robert Wurster

Pg 148 Martha bed: Frewil, Inc. Los Angeles, CA
www.frewil.com

About the author

Sharon's interest in the healing power of homes began in 1994 in response to a debilitating and chronic illness. She studied with numerous teachers, including Carol Bridges, Karen Kingston, and the Geomancy Education Organization, to gain a broad understanding of multiple approaches to the art of feng shui. Since then, Sharon has worked with homeowners, designers, architects, and businesses to create harmonious environments in settings as diverse as studio apartments, multimillion-dollar estates, classrooms, and hospitals.

Experienced in both interior design and feng shui, Sharon emphasizes the energetics of every design choice. She draws upon many healing modalities, including NLP, chakras, color therapy, Qi Gong, and meditation when customizing traditional feng shui approaches to support the needs of the individual. Her intention is to provide an opportunity for people to become more intimately aware of their relationship with their living spaces and learn to use those spaces to heal and grow.

Index